S0-AJQ-323

LANDSAILING...from RC Models to the Big Ones

By George C. Siposs

MANNIX

TAB BOOKS

Blue Ridge Summit, Pa. 17214

FIRST EDITION

FIRST PRINTING—JUNE 1973

Copyright © 1973 by TAB BOOKS

Printed in the United States
of America

Reproduction or publication of the content in any manner, without express permission of the publisher, is prohibited. No liability is assumed with respect to the use of the information herein.

Hardbound Edition: International Standard Book No. 0-8306-3659-5

Paperbound Edition: International Standard Book No. 0-8306-2659-X

Library of Congress Card Number: 73-78196

Preface

A new star is shining brightly on the horizon of American "hobby" sports: landsailing! This is a clean, ecology-oriented sport whose devotees are gentle people out for a relaxing good time. Yet, when the starting flag drops they become fierce competitors, for landsailing, as sailing on water, can be as relaxing or demanding as the participant wishes it to be.

Equipped with three wheels, a sail, and a seat for the pilot, the landsailing vehicle is deceptively simple. On the other hand, it can be quite sophisticated, capable of attaining land speeds of nearly a hundred miles an hour.

While there are literally thousands of landsailors (the people) and just as many landsailers (the "boats"), there is no other book devoted exclusively to the sport. It is so new that your encyclopedia does not devote any space to it, and there is no universal agreement yet on whether to call it landsailing, land yachting, desert sailing, or whatever. The people who sail may be called pilots, yachtsmen, skippers, or landsailors. Sailing techniques, racing events, and construction methods are becoming so involved that a very real need exists to provide one simple reference source for them all. The novice wants to learn everything there is to know about it while the expert seeks a reference source. I hope that this work will fill both needs.

And now a word to the casual reader. Perhaps you have just picked this book off the bookstand—perhaps the title got you intrigued. Perhaps you are looking for a fabulous new pastime. Whatever the reason, I hope that by the time you read through to the last chapter you will have felt the wind in your face, your hand will have strained to hold an imaginary rope, and you will have applied some "body english" as your foot bore down on the steering bar.

I was aided immensely by many people and companies who so generously supplied me with illustrative material. My special gratitude goes to Frank Jayne, Don Moyer, Don Rypinski, Dick Dodd, William Sarns, Steve Kulik, Mel Holman, William Connell, Warren Darress, Tim Fredman, Raymond Ruge, John Young, Robert Ashlock, and John Schindler, plus many others whom I learned to know and whose friendship I will appreciate throughtout the years to come. Special acknowledgment is due the following companies for giving permission to use parts of their literature and illustrations: Lighthouse Landsailers, Honker Landsailers, Windbuggy Mfg. Co., NuSport Mfg. Co., and Las Vegas News Bureau.

George C. Siposs

Contents

History of Landsailing

Man is lazy. Ever since the invention of the wheel he has been wracking his brain trying to find a method of propelling the wheel so that he may be able to sit comfortably in a chair yet move along at a fair clip. Hitching a horse to the wagon was not too satisfactory because it required the cooperation of another living thing. Of course there is that kind of pleasure in coasting downhill in a wagon.

But hills are short; so when one wants to cover greater distances, a different method of locomotion has to be employed.

A SPORT WITH A PAST

Sail powered rafts and boats have been with us for thousands of years, perhaps because their method of operation was copied from a wind-driven leaf on the surface of a quiet lake or river. Constructing a wind-driven, wheeled, steerable vehicle requires a particular skill and inventiveness because one can find no counterpart in nature. Yet, as long past as 2600 years ago, the Chinese had wind-propelled war chariots that were large enough to carry 30 warriors.

Paintings found on the walls of ancient Egyptian tombs depict sailing vehicles racing on the banks of the Nile.

An anonymous engraving in an ancient book shows a picture of four-wheeled landsailers on a sandy beach. The date is 1600 and the passengers in the clumsy vehicle are Maurice of Nassau, Prince of Orange and his friends. Resembling a huge flatbed wagon with spoked wooden wheels, these four-wheeled forerunners of today's spindly fliers were designed in the late 1500s by Dutch mathematician Simon Stevin. When the wind blew directly from behind the wagon, it would roll along at about 25 mph. But when the wind came from the side there was no push power available because the sails were of the then traditional square-rigged construction—the type seen on Columbus' ships and pirates' frigates.

Another early landsailer is recorded in 1834 (L'Eolienne) in Paris, France. This was also a four-wheeled cart, with two masts sporting six sails, capable of carrying 15 or 20 people.

If you look in the archives of the early American West you will find records of an ambitious group of entrepreneurs who lived in Kansas City around 1853. Encouraged by the optimistic reports coming back from the recently conquered Western territory, and foreseeing a great demand for material goods, these people planned on loading merchandise on wind-powered wagons. With the cost of transportation extremely low, great profits seemed to be possible. A company was formed and stock was sold. Then came the big day and the stockholders got aboard the land yacht. Amid cheers, bands and caps thrown high in the air, the wagon rolled out of town only to meet with misfortune in a short while. The venture came to a sudden windless end.

A gentleman who was aptly named "Windwagon Smith" (we have also found other references to the same man as Windwagon Jones and Windwagon Thomas) attached sails to his trusty conestoga wagon to aid his westward emigration. Apparently this venture was successful.

A short newspaper report mentions the appearance of a land yacht in Muroc, California in 1902. This particular model must have had very revolutionary design ideas incorporated because its speed was a then hair-raising 60 miles per hour. Just about at the same time the famous French aviator Louis Bleriot (first man to successfully fly from France to England over the La Mans channel) constructed a four-wheeled

landsailer bearing a striking resemblance to those of the modern era.

The first international competition on record was held in Belgium, where the names on the starting lines seemed to be taken from the Who's Who of early aviation: Santos-Dumont, Duvoisin, Bleriot, and others. It is perhaps for this reason that today landsailing is one of the most popular sports where the flat beaches become nearly one mile wide at low tide.

Wishing to provide American sportsmen with a competitive machine, a group of enterprising men had designed and built a utility landsailer in 1937. Messrs. Aarel, Lodge, and Genitt actually built a rig in the basement workshops of the Detroit Evening News and named it, appropriately, the "DN" (for Detroit News). Today, the same basic design is the most popular model to be found anywhere, and thousands of replicas have been built in the United States and Europe.

An illustrated article in the July 14, 1941 issue of the now defunct **Life** magazine describes sailing activities on a Sea Island, Ga. beach. These landsailers look quite modern even by today's standards. **Look** magazine (March 29, 1938) described the adventures of members of the "Ad Astra" club (mostly RAF officers), who sailed their craft on the hard sands near Abu-Sueir about 65 miles north of Cairo. The recorded speed attained by those landsailers was about 44 miles per hour.

LANDSAILING POPULARIZED

Back in 1959, Don Rypinski decided to build a sail-powered wheeled vehicle simply "to harness the wind." Don did not know of any other activities in this sport nor had he ever seen a similar craft before. His design was an instant success. One breezy day as he was sailing along on the gentle dunes of a California beach, he met a young Canadian, Ian Critchley, who had recently married and was at that time looking for a job. The two of them built another model and showed it to a local industrialist, Bud Hulst, who advanced $1000 to the two young men to build a production model. This was shown at a local boat show, where the public immediately took a liking to it. Another Californian, John Schindler, bought this model, redesigned it, and made it a new-class landsailer which he aptly named "Sandsailer Class." It was later improved and redesigned to become the still popular "Desert Dart" class sailer. In 1964 Don Rypinski began corresponding with European sportsman devoted to landsailing. The sport began to bring in more and more enthusiasts as John Schindler organized the National Sand Sailer Association at Eagle Rock, Calif. John had built and sold more than 150 sailers and through his efforts the first American landsailing racing organization had begun.

In 1967 this avid group received a 12-page invitation from a French colonel, Jean du Boucher for an 1800-mile trans-Sahara landsailer "safari." Three Americans went on this unforgettable trip; their adventures are described in the November 1967 issue of National Geographic magazine.

Enter Frank Jayne and Dick Dodd, two more Californians who took it upon themselves to fully popularize landsailing by producing low-cost units that require no more than average skill to assemble and sail. Beginning in 1971 the companies founded by these people began turning out vehicles that are the Chevies and MGs of this old-new sport.

YOU AND LANDSAILING

How about you? I have found that most people know of someone who has tried landsailing at one time or another. Not very serious efforts, maybe, but interesting ones at that. In many cases, I have talked to people who, with a gleam in their

eyes, recalled the days in their childhood when they attached a simple sail to a small wagon (or baby carriage) and managed to harness the wind for short distances.

Didn't you ever try to hold a rudimentary sail in your hand as you stood on your skates on that windswept, hard-frozen lake? Didn't you secretly wish to travel with Phineas Fogg and his servant Passpartout in Jules Verne's "Around the World in 80 Days" as they sailed along the American prairies in their efforts to beat the deadline?

All About Sails

Somewhere back in the history of mankind there happened an event that had almost as much to do with our development as the discovery of fire.

There was a dry leaf floating on top of a lake and, as a puff of wind came by, the leaf was pushed along by it. The same wind brought more and larger leaves along and, as our caveman ancestors were able to observe with great interest, the larger the leaf was (the more "bite" it offered to the wind), the faster it floated.

THE EARLY SAILOR

As man is able to correlate seemingly unrelated subjects, our caveman ancestor soon figured that there may be something worth investigating here. He was soon at work making a frame from wooden twigs on which he stretched a light animal skin. With the help of a heavier piece of wood he was able to attach this elementary sail to the top of his dugout canoe. To his delight, the wind pushed his boat gently along the surface of the lake. Soon he built bigger and better sails to power bigger and faster boats.

And so, for thousands of years, our civilization was being shaped partially by sailboats. Warships carried warriors for an attack on an unsuspecting enemy, barges carried grain along the Nile for great distances. The Pinta brought Columbus to the New World, clippers brought oriental goods to the wealthy merchants of England, Pirates and missionaries traveled to faraway lands. The cost of traveling was low. The initial cost of the boat was the only major investment after which one only had to pay for his own food. Since the wind was free, fuel was seldom a problem.

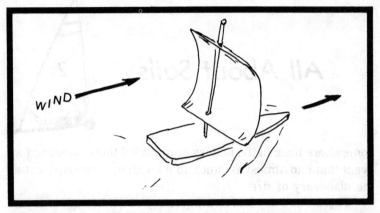

Fig. 2-1. A square-rigged toy sailboat illustrates the point that these sails can only provide motive force when the wind is blowing directly from behind.

THE EVOLUTION OF DESIGN

There was one hang-up with the early ships. They were "square-rigged," which means that their sails were square shaped and supported along the centerlines, as shown in Fig. 2-1. With this kind of sail, the wind must be behind the ship for propulsion. The ancient mariners had to rely on tradewinds and other predictable air currents that would carry them to the desired destination.

Less than a hundred years ago, civilized man discovered how to make use of the triangular sail, attached to its mast along one of the sides only. This sail can be made to resemble an airplane wing in cross section to provide forward push regardless of which direction the wind comes from.

A **complete** understanding of the triangular sail is the treasured property of a chosen few, but most modern sailors understand how the sail works in a general way and can manipulate it by feel and experience. Landsailing being a fairly new sport, there are only a few experts who **really** know how sails work at speeds much higher than a sailboat attains.

EXPERIMENTING WITH MODELS

Place a wooden wedge on top of a toy wheeled vehicle on a table top and exert a downward pressure on it, as shown in

Fig. 2-2. If you push straight down you will find that either the wedge will move forward off the toy, or the toy (and wedge) will begin to roll. You are pushing in a vertical plane, yet it moves horizontally. If the wedge has a 45-degree angle, the distance moved by the vehicle is exactly equal to the distance moved by the roller. The forward movement of the vehicle depends on the angle of the wedge. The analogy of the wedge to sailing is shown in Fig. 2-3.

A MATTER OF SAIL ANGLE

To make the example more closely resemble a sailboat or landsailer, place the block on the vehicle in a sideways position as shown in Fig. 2-4. Now the wedge surface resembles a sail and the pressure exerted against it will take the place of the wind. Again, you will find that the vehicle will move forward when the "wind" blows sideways.

As you use a smaller and smaller wedge angle, you will find that the vehicle will want to slip sideways on the table. If you now equip your experimental vehicle with rubber-tired wheels, you will find that the vehicle will tend to grip the surface. You will be able to use a smaller wedge angle and, most importantly, for a given distance of "wind" travel, the distance traveled by the vehicle will be longer.

The practical implication of this experiment should be clearer now. If we let the distance traveled by the "wind" be

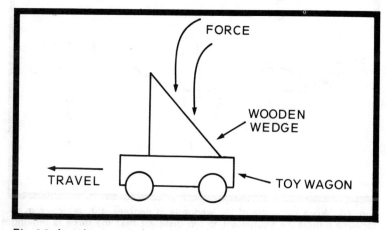

Fig. 2-2. A wedge mounted on a simple vehicle illustrates the principle of how wind provides a motive force.

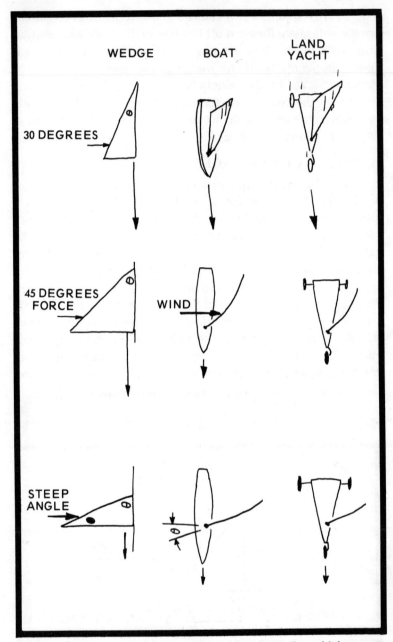

Fig. 2-3. When the angle of the wedge is 45 degrees, the vehicle moves forward a distance equivalent to the distance that the force is moving through. When the angle is 30 degrees the vehicle moves further than the movement of the force.

proportional to the speed of the real wind, and, if we let the distance traveled by the vehicle be proportional to the landsailer, we will see that a 45-degree sail setting will limit the speed of the vehicle to the speed of the wind (neglecting experimental errors, unevenness of surfaces, friction in the bearings, etc.). And if we carry out out thinking further it will become evident that when the angle of the sail is closer and closer to being at a right angle (90 degrees) to the wind, we should be able to sail much faster than the speed of the prevailing wind.

Friction and Sailing

Friction between the vehicle and the supporting surface (e.g., hull and water, wheels and runway, skates and ice) is the most critical factor in the equation. Frictional drag on the skin of a boat hull can be very great. For this reason boats can seldom go twice as fast as the speed of the prevailing wind. Landsailers, on the other hand, have bearinged wheels and well inflated tires so their frictional resistance is low. Most landsailers are able to travel at speeds much more than twice that of the wind. Iceboats, with only minimal resistance on their skates, can travel three times faster than the wind.

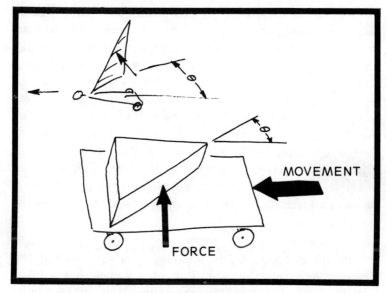

Fig. 2-4. A horizontal wedge simulates an actual sail.

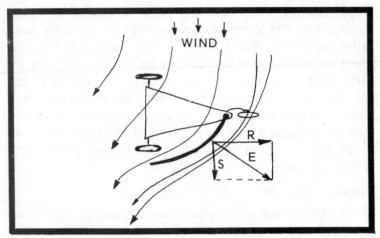

Fig. 2-5. The wind, flowing around the sail, combines into one resultant force.

By the way, if you happen to have a model landsailer, the above experiments can be performed very nicely. Make sure that the surface is smooth, set the sail to a 45-degree angle and use your fingertip as wind. Your fingertip will slide along the smooth Dacron cloth and the landsailer will roll effortlessly.

A Combination of Forces

Figure 2-5 illustrates various positions of the sail and vehicle in relation to the wind. Arrow E represents the **total** wind energy thrust. The direction of the arrow is at a 90-degree angle to the sail. This is because the only component of wind that the sail will feel must be at a right angle to the canvas; otherwise, the wind can be considered to be "slipping off" along the sail. The actual direction of the wind is shown by arrow S; this is the vector responsible for making sailboats heel over. The combined effect of the two vectors is represented by arrow R, which is called the **resultant**. As an example, the force acting on an airplane wing —lift, drag, thrust, and weight—is the resultant force that supports the plane.

As long as a sail-bearing wheeled vehicle has very little frictional resistance, it will roll along even with the slightest pressure exerted on the sail. But if the vehicle has a lot of friction (rotational as well as translational), it will tend to tip over rather than move forward. You can simulate this easily with your model: Tie a string to the end of the vehicle and tie a small weight to the string. Let this weight drag on the surface of the table...now the vehicle has a lot of friction which resists movement. It is easy to understand now that, since a sailboat has a lot of hull frictional resistance, it will heel over easily rather than speed forward. A landsailer, on the other hand, has relatively little resistance and it will go a lot faster before it will tend to heel over.

True vs Apparent Winds

The arrow-vector representations of the motive forces acting on the sail are really only valid with the sailer standing still. The moment the vehicle begins to move, there is a new entity to contend with. This is called the **apparent wind**. To understand what this means we have to go back to basics.

Imagine yourself standing on the starting line ready to go, but somebody is holding your landsailer firmly so that it cannot move. You will feel the wind coming from your **side**. For example, the right side of your face will feel the breeze. Now imagine that suddenly the wind has died off completely. Your helper pushes your vehicle forward and now you feel a breeze on the **front** of your face. The breeze you have felt coming from the side was the **true** wind while the wind you have felt coming from the front was **motion** wind. Motion wind is what you feel when you are riding a bike or driving in an open convertible.

The sail "feels" the same wind as you do. On the starting line it feels the wind coming from the side. At high speeds, should the true wind suddenly stop, the sail will feel the motion wind and be slowed by it. Water sailors actually use this phenomenon to slow their boats down when approaching a dock. They spread the sails at a 90-degree angle to the boat so that the sails will brake the ship's forward travel.

Few things in nature happen by themselves. And so it is with true wind and motion wind. The sail usually feels a combination of the two, and it is their resultant (the combination of their two vectors) that counts. Thus, at the start, the sail is subjected to true wind only. As you begin to move, the motion wind combines with the true wind and the resulting apparent wind now seems to be coming more and more from the front. In order to maintain speed you pull in your sail so that it still presents the same angle to the apparent wind. At high speeds the sail is pulled in quite tight because the apparent wind seems to be coming from dead ahead or nearly so.

Let us consider a true wind of 12 mph coming directly from the right. As the vehicle reaches exactly 12 mph, the combined "true" and "motion" wind forces produce an apparent wind from a direction of 45 degrees from the front. This is because when you combine two equal winds at a 90-degree angle, their resultant will have an angle of 45 degrees. The apparent velocity of the 12 mph wind coming from a 45-degree angle is 17 mph.

When your ground speed reaches 24 mph while the wind is maintained at 12 mph, the apparent wind will shift to an angle of about 27 degrees and a speed of 26 mph. At a ground speed of 36 mph (remember that three times wind speed is possible on a landsailer), the apparent wind will reach 40 mph with an apparent direction of 18 degrees. In sailing language, even though you are "reaching" with respect to the true wind, your sails are trimmed hard on the apparent wind. Thus, the apparent wind is the combination of the true wind and the motion generated by your own speed.

Telltails

It may be difficult for you to visualize the air flowing past your sail but there is an easy way to make the streamlines appear visible. Most experienced landsailors sew small tufts of cotton or strips of canvas to the sides of their sail. As the air rushes past the sail it drags the "telltails" with it. When the airstream is smooth, the telltails are flat against the canvas. When the sail is not set properly and one side "stalls" (i.e. the air does not follow the sail contour faithfully and creates turbulences instead) the telltails will flutter and bounce around aimlessly. The aim of a good sailor is to keep the telltails on both sides of the sail lying flat against the canvas.

THE CONSTRUCTION OF SAILS

In the old days, sails used to be made from canvas. This was a good strong material, but if it was not cared for properly, mildew and rot could destroy the sail.

Material

Modern sails are made from synthetic materials. Dupont's Dacron is the most popular material. Dacron is made from polyester fibers extruded from molten material into solidified and pliable fibers that have no lint or frayed ends. When the fibers are cross-woven into flat cloth, the resulting material is very smooth and close-meshed so that air will not penetrate it. It is strong, relatively tear-resistant, and completely mildew-proof.

Fabrication

Heavy-duty sewing machines are used to sew the material into the desired shape. The form is cut from roll stock by means of scissors or a hot knife which automatically sears the ends of the fibers to prevent fraying. Sails are cut, tailored, and sewn in huge rooms with smooth flat floors, as shown in Fig. 2-6. The outline of the sail may be taped or painted on the floor so that duplication is easily accomplished. The sewing machines are located at floor level, but the operator sits in a hole below floor level so that sewing is accomplished without cloth stretching.

Configuration

The basic shape of the sail (Fig. 2-7) is a triangle. Two of the sides of the triangle are rectilinear. These sides are defined and constrained by the mast and the boom so there is not much one can do to change their shape. The third side, however, is usually curved on the outside of the imaginary triangular outline. This section is called the "roach."

The function of the roach is to further enlarge the actual sail area (especially at the top to catch over-the-ground breeze) without having to resort to a higher mast which would

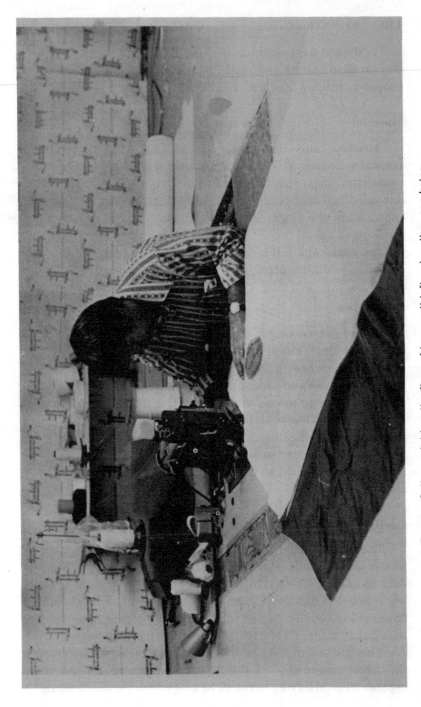

Fig. 2-6. Sails are laid on the floor of huge sail lofts when they are being sewn by master sailmakers.

make the vehicle top-heavy. The problem with the roach is that it has no visible means of support and it would tend to flop out (without catching the wind) were it not tied to the rest of the sail by battens. Battens are flat, thin strips of wood or fiber glass inserted into pockets in the sail. Any pressure exerted by the wind at the tip of a batten (along the outside edge of the roach) is automatically transferred to the rest of the sail. Thus, in spite of its curved outline, the sail still acts as if it were solidly supported. In addition, the flat battens conform to the shape of the sail even when it is severely deflected to either side by the wind and caused to conform to an airfoil shape.

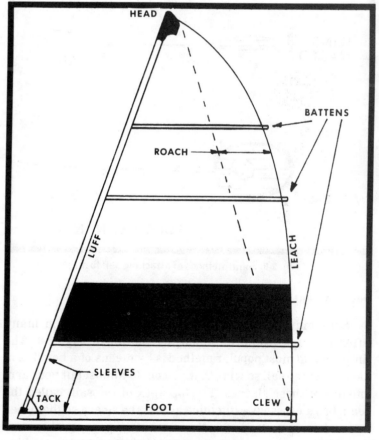

Fig. 2-7. Sail terminology.

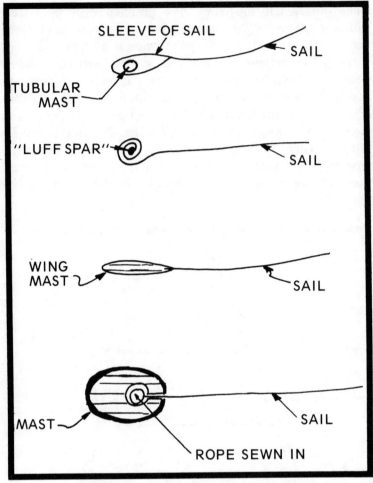

Fig. 2-8. Some methods of attaching sail to mast.

Development

Sails may be fastened to the mast and boom in many different ways, some of which are shown in Fig. 2-8. The simplest and most popular method is by means of a hemline at the edge of the sail so wide that you could almost put your arm into one of these sleeves. The top apex of the sail, called the head, has a crosswise stitchline across the sleeve so that when the sail is mounted over the mast (by passing the mast through the sleeve from the bottom up(THIS CROSS -stitching rests on the extreme tip of the mast. Thus, the mast actually supports the weight of the sail and prevents it from slipping down. The boom may be passed through a similar sleeve. At the forward bottom apex of the sail, the canvas is cut away so that the sleeves do not touch each other. This permits one to fasten the boom to the mast by one of several methods.

Another popular method of fastening the sail to the mast is by a rope sewn into the edge of the sail and having a T-shaped groove routed into the mast along its entire length. This groove, being in the center of the mast, does not weaken the wood appreciably but it allows the rope to pass inside the wooden mast.

The most desirable attachment method is one which presents very little discontinuity at the point where the sail and mast meet. (This is achieved to a certain extent by the sleeve method.) Thus, the cross section of the mast shows a slight thickening at the front and resembles an airfoil found in bird and airplane wings. For this reason, the very efficient masts whose cross section resembles an airfoil are called "wing masts."

When the prevailing wind is too strong, you can reduce the size of your sail by one of several methods. One is to rotate the mast so that it furls up a portion of the sail. This is called the "luff spar" method. Another method is to lower the sail so that it does not reach to the top of the mast, and furl the excess on the boom. Whatever the case, it is most convenient to have "reefing" points on the canvas located so that when the canvas strips (sewn to the canvas) are used to tie up the furled-in sail, the remaining sail area matches the new, desired reduced sail area exactly. In this manner, no tedious remeasuring is required every time you change down to a smaller sail size.

Sail Area. It is relatively simple to measure the sail area by the classic formula: height times half base (Fig. 2-9). When the leach of the sail is excessive, careful measurements have to be performed. For instance, the ISA iceboating rules state that the leach line must be no more than 12 inches from an imaginary line connecting the tip of the mast and the aft tip of

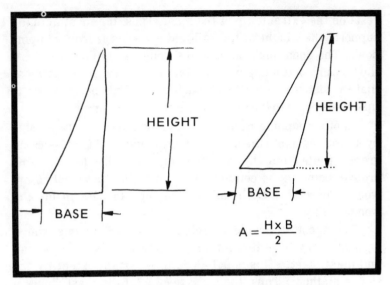

$$A = \frac{H \times B}{2}$$

Fig. 2-9. Area of sail equals height times base divided by two.

the boom. As a rule, every club has an official sail measurer whose duties are to measure and certify the sail areas and to affix a stamp, with his signature, to every sail registered for racing. The stamp usually bears the sail triangular height and base dimensions, the year of testing, and the signature of the official.

Sail Life. Actually, sails seem to assume an identity of their own. The canvas has some "life" to it, meaning that it may shrink or stretch due to the tremendous windloads on it. A 20 mph wind may exert as much as 250 pounds of brute pressure on a 75 square foot sail. A sail which works perfectly in one type of wind may be quite useless under different wind conditions. A sail may behave splendidly in a 30 mph dry wind in the desert but it may be a dud at 15 mph winds on the damp beach. A popular complaint among landsailors: "My sail went dead." (After jall, there is no engine to blame.)

Among some of the more common misconceptions is: the more sail you have, the faster you go. While adding sail in very light breezes will make you go faster, adding sail in a powerful wind may actually slow you down. For most efficient sailing, you pull the sail in tight; in high winds this tends to tip the vehicle, so you let the sail out somewhat. A smaller sail can be pulled in tighter to provide more driving force.

Curvature. The curvature of the sail (Fig. 2-10) is called "draft." A full sail has a deep belly to it when sheeted (pulled) in hard, while a flat sail has relatively little curvature. For light air and low speeds a full sail is desirable and vice versa.

The same theory holds for aircraft as shown in Fig. 2-11. A fast airplane has a thin, flat wing cross section while a slow plane has a thicker airfoil with more curvature to it. For this reason, sails used for landsailers tend to be more flat than the sails used for sailboats. When the constant pressure has stretched the canvas to the point where it is impossible to make it sufficiently flat (i.e. it has a constant deep belly to it), it is called a "blown sail." One can adjust the fullness or draft by adjusting the downhaul. Increasing the tension on the downhaul moves the draft forward. Outhaul tension and batten tension also affect draft. However it is too easy to spend

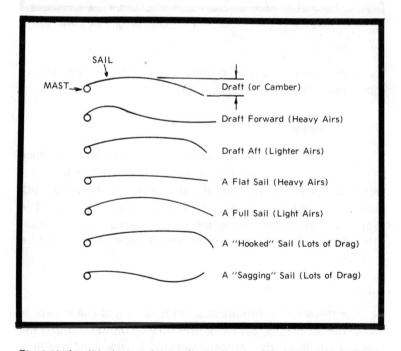

Fig. 2-10. A sail is deployed according to the condition of the wind. These are common shapes a sail experiences.

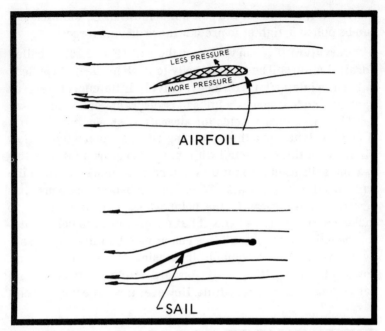

Fig. 2-11. Note the similarity between airflows around an airfoil and a sail.

hours adjusting and only minutes sailing if you get overly concerned about the perfect shape.

Mast Resilience

If the mast has some springiness in it, it will also introduce a new factor into an already complex equation. When the mast points directly into the wind the forces will be equal on both sides of the sail. This causes the sail to flutter, or "luff." The rapid back-and-forth movement of the canvas has potential deleterious effects because of intense stresses and should be avoided.

Applying Wind Forces

For design calculations of a landsailer, it is convenient to locate the theoretical center of pressure on the sail. This is the point at which all the forces generated by the wind are concentrated. To find the pressure of the wind **per unit area,** you should consult the table of wind and its effects, Fig. 2-12. To find the total force of the wind, multiply the tabular figure by the area of the sail. For example, a 10 mph wind has a pressure of 1.5 lb per square foot (1.5 psf) sail. The total pressure of is the product of the area times the pressure per unit area. In our case (say, if the sail is a 75-square-footer) 112.5 lb total. This is evenly distributed along the entire area of the sail but it could be replaced by one single force of 112.5 lb acting at the center of pressure (cp). The cp of a triangular sail is located as shown in Fig. 2-13. Draw a line between any apex of the sail (say, the aft tip of the boom) and the center of the opposite side (the center of the mast part of the sail). Draw another line from any other apex (say, the top of the mast) and connect it with the center of the opposite side (the center of the boom). Where these two lines intersect is the cp.

As the wind "looks" at an upright sail, it "sees" the entire sail area. But, when the vehicle heels over, the wind sees only a small area. It is for this reason that much of the driving force is lost when the landsailing vehicle heels over. The wind simply spills out from the sail over its top.

As shown in Fig. 2-14, the more the sail is tipped over, the more this power loss becomes. Thus, while it may look very exciting when a landsailor tips his vehicle over and "two-wheels" it, he is really not increasing his speed. The fellow with the upright vehicle will travel faster.

On the other hand, the wind-spilling action serves as a safety valve at times when you are caught by a sudden gust of wind and the vehicle wants to tip over. You will find that when this happens (Fig. 2-16), it will soon right itself because the wind pressure is automatically reduced to a safe point.

Sails and their theory can be calculated to a fine degree, but there is simply no substitute for empirical methods and long years of experience.

It has been found by experienced landsailer designers that it is best to make the mast in such a way that the center of pressure is directly above the center of gravity of the vehicle itself with the driver on board. The center of gravity is placed just ahead of the rear axle as shown in Fig. 2-15. This results in the following weight distribution: front wheel 20 percent, each

CONDITION OF WATER	WIND FORCE	WIND TERM	WIND SPEED, mph	INTERNAT. WIND FORCE UNIT	BOAT SPEED, mph	LANDSAILER SPEED mph	ICEBOAT SPEED mph
ripple patches	0.1-0.5	light airs	1-3	1	1	3-6	10
water surface covered with ripples	0.5-1	light breeze	4-7	2	3	8-14	15
waves begin	1-2	gentle breeze	8-12	3	6	16-30	30
longer waves	2-3	moder. breeze	13-18	4	10	25-40	50
few whitecaps	3-4	fresh breeze	19-24	5	15	20-60	65
many whitecaps	4-6	strong breeze	25-31	6	20	60	90

Fig. 2-12. Table of wind and its effects.

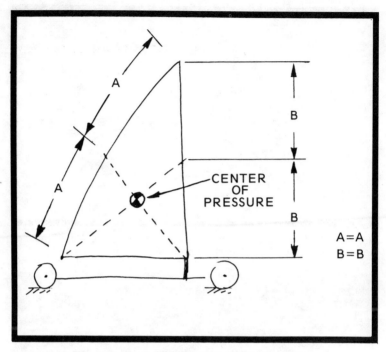

Fig. 2-13. How to calculate the center of pressure.

rear wheel 40 percent. (Note that when you lift a wheel this immediately becomes 20 percent on the front wheel and 80 percent on the remaining rear wheel.) This weight distribution keeps the front wheel from being heavily loaded; it is easily steerable and will not dig in or produce a spinout. Also, the more weight the rear tires are carrying, the more stable the vehicle will be for straight running at high speeds.

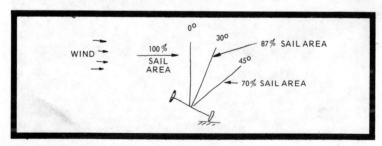

Fig. 2-14. When the sail is tilted, only a fraction of its area can be used to propel the landsailer.

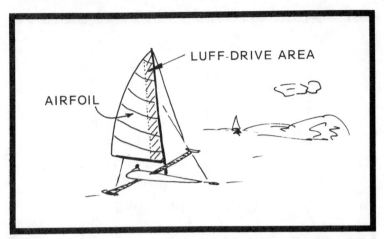

Fig. 2-15. The forward one-third of the sail (luff-drive area) does most of the work; the rest of the sail (airfoil) provides smooth airflow.

Fig. 2-16. This landsailer is "popping a wheelie." A spectacular maneuver but it actually slows you down.

How to Sail

You may find it helpful to rig up an elementary sailing trainer in your own backyard. Two broomsticks with a sheet of canvas nailed to them, plus a rope attached to the end of the "boom," may be all you need.

STATIC LESSONS

Before you do anything study the positional terminology diagram of Fig. 3-1. It will aid immeasurably in understanding directions for controlling your vehicle.

As you read the instructions, try to visualize why and what is being done, what results it will produce, and what could happen if you did not follow the instructions. If you happen to

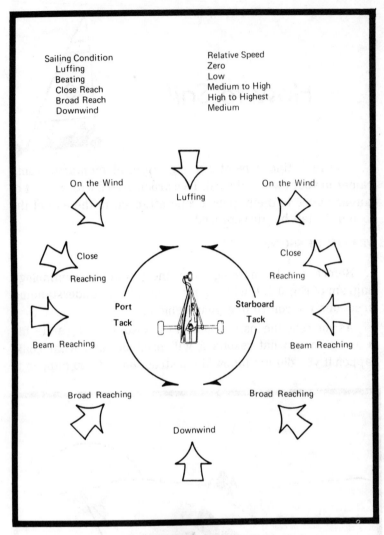

Fig. 3-1. Sailing terminology is illustrated.

have a landsailer, take it out to a nearby parking lot on a nice balmy day with a gentle breeze blowing. Put chocks under the wheels, strap yourself in the seat, and read on. Do not try to make your vehicle move until you have actually completed reading this entire chapter.

Point your landsailer into the wind for the next several steps. (Pointing into the wind means that the front wheel and the mast are between you and the source of the wind.) If sand is blowing in the air, you may even want to put on your goggles.

Put your feet on the steering bar and grab the rope leading to the sail in both hands. Now, pull the sail in hard! See, you didn't go very far! This is intended as a lesson. The sheet is your accelerator but you don't necessarily "tromp on it" to make your vehicle go. No matter how frustrated you may get at first and want to pull hard on the sheet, just say to yourself: **IF IN DOUBT, LET SAIL OUT!** A light touch on the sheet will generally have more satisfying results, particularly in light breezes. Save your muscles for high speed and good breezes.

Trimming the Sail

It may help to think of the sail as the wing of an airplane or soaring bird. And there is a great deal of similarity: land-sailers, birds, and airplanes employ "lift." Lift, in turn, is caused by the air flowing on **both** sides of the wing or sail at the same time with different velocities or speeds of flow. The faster flow is on the side toward which the sail is moving, causing the pressure to be lower. This is generally the leeward side, further from the wind. The slower flow is on the windward side where the higher pressure exists. Thus the sail is "caught" between the high pressure on the windward side and the low pressure on the leeward. Continually it tries to move itself out of the high pressure behind it and into the low pressure ahead of it.

The sheet has the single purpose of controlling this air pressure system. If you were always to sail in the same direction at the same speed with the wind strength and direction constant, you could "set it and forget it." However, as the vehicle's direction and speed and the **wind** direction and speed change constantly, the sheet must be constantly adjusted. Mastering sheet control is the most important part of getting your landsailer to perform well.

Telltails. Again, before you sail away for your first ride, place a couple of strips of bright-colored, lightweight ribbon on the sail. Attach one on each side with tape about 10 inches back from the mast and 18 inches up from the boom.

Now set your full-rigged vehicle so that its direction makes an angle of 60 degrees to 70 degrees with the direction of the wind. Watch how the sail behaves as you adjust its angle to the wind indicator. The two ribbons, or telltails, will give you an indication of airflow.

With no pull on the sheet, the sail and boom will align themselves with the direction of the wind to equalize the pressure on both sides of the sail. The sail will flutter and the boom will bounce around. The telltails will flutter randomly with the sail, much like a flag.

Pinching. Next, gently pull the sheet in, just to the point where the sail is barely full for "drawing." While the windward or nearer telltail may still flutter a bit, the leeward or further telltail will stream smoothly back along the sail—perhaps with a little motion as the air swirls and eddies across the sail. Also look at the luff of the sail, where the sail joins the mast. If you have not pulled the sail in too far, its luff will still have a tendency to flutter or bubble from the leeward side near the mast. The sail is said to be "pinching" when this flutter occurs at the luff. It means that some of the high pressure air from the windward side is leaking around the mast to the leeward, where it can do you no good.

Bring the sheet in some more—say another five or ten degrees on the boom. You will notice that the pinching disappears and, if you haven't sheeted in too far already, both telltails are streaming smoothly back along the sail surface. If you were moving, this would be about the proper place to set the sail. Notice that the sheet is not yet pulled in as tightly as possible and that the boom still makes an angle somewhere between the direction of the landsailer and the direction of the wind. The sail is lifting, or drawing, and is said to be "trimmed."

Overtrimming. Next, with the wheels still chocked, overtrim the sail by bringing the sheet in tightly. Look up at the sail. The aft ends of the battens are probably hooked toward the windward. They are "dragging" the air flow. This would cause you to slow down. Look at the telltails. The windward one should be streaming well, but the leeward one will be lazily (or even vigorously) drifting and fluttering around. This tells you that there is little or no smooth airflow on the leeward side of the sail. In this condition the breeze, if it is strong enough, will attempt to lift the windward wheel off the ground.

It takes some overtrimming to lift the wheel when you are actually going. If you intend to race, you should remember that lifting the wheel (which is great fun itself) usually happens at the expense of speed because it requires overtrimming. Overtrimming results in drag and side thrust which would slow you down. This also should tell you how to get the wheel back on the ground if you don't want it up there: ease the sheet out.

Try this while the wheels are still chocked: overtrim the sheet and let it out to the well trimmed position quickly and smoothly. You should feel your landsailer surge forward against the chocks momentarily. Smoothly and rhythmically done in actual sailing, this "pumping" can give you bursts of acceleration and increased speed.

Repeat the above steps with your vehicle still chocked, but headed at other angles to the wind direction. You will notice that every heading requires a different boom angle or sheeting position for stalling, trim, and pinching. As you increase the angle between you and the wind, notice that the boom angle for proper trim increases also. Finally, as you reach the "downwind" condition, with the wind coming from nearly or directly behind you, the sail will only be either in a stall condition (way out) which is correct downwind, or it will be overtrimmed (sheeted in too far). Downwind you should attempt to present as much sail area to the wind as possible—up to the point where the luff of the sail begins to flutter.

Jibing. Notice also that as you pass through the dead downwind position (wind directly aft), the boom will tack, or be taken to the other side. The sail has "jibed." In actual sailing, the sail and boom can be assisted in the jibe by a

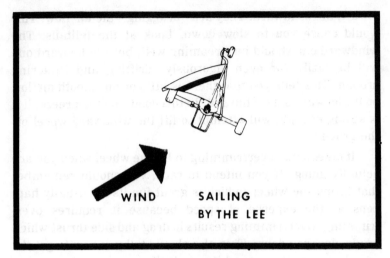

WIND

SAILING
BY THE LEE

Fig. 3-2. Sailing by the lee.

smooth motion of sheeting in and out. This makes jibing less violent.

If you are sailing with the wind more than dead aft without jibing, you will be "sailing by the lee," the condition pictured in Fig. 3-2. There are two good reasons to avoid sailing by the lee. First, it will be slower than sailing with proper trim (on the other tack). Second, it may lead to a violent (and possibly gearbusting) unintentional jibe. An intentional and smoothly carried out jibe is a desirable and often exciting maneuver, while a violent and unintentional jibe is the mark of a poor sailor.

The purpose of smooth in-and-out sheeting during the jibe is to prevent the boom from lifting excessively during the jibe. Violent lifting of the boom can result in parts of the sail on opposite sides of the mast, snapped battens, and even torn batten pockets. Should this sort of mess ever occur, you should immediately head back into the wind—back through the direction you turned from and "unwind" it. This may require getting out of the machine and physically moving the front wheel around to windward and possibly parking, by laying your landsailer over with the **head of the mast on the ground**. Control your jibes, or use a "boom vang" to hold the boom down during a jibe.

Luffing up. Let's assume you have gone through all the previous steps while chocked. Keep changing your heading a few degrees at a time with the same direction or rotation with respect to the wind. When you have reached a heading angle of about 60 degrees or less on the other tack from which you started, you will notice that you can no longer completely trim the sail to avoid pinching. This will be even more apparent as you approach a "head to wind" condition when the sail flutters uncontrollably. If you were going from this 60-degree position on either tack to "head to wind" while actually sailing, you would be "luffing up," as illustrated in Fig. 3-3.

This kills the speed, since the pressure on the sail vanishes. It is the simplest method of stopping, provided you have plenty of rolling distance to go straight into the wind. Remember, if you turn off either way, the pressure will once again resume on the sail, unless you let the sheet out until the whole sail flutters. Luffing is the most elementary stopping procedure. (Flipping is perhaps more elementary but not recommended as good practice.)

Tacking. If, instead of luffing to stop as in the previous step, you had steered smoothly to put the wind from about 60 degrees on one tack to 60 degrees on the other tack (Fig. 3-4), you are said to have "tacked." The boom will move (more or less violently, depending on the wind strength) from one side of center to the other.

You can see the difference between tacking and jibing. In a tacking maneuver such as that shown in Fig. 3-5, the **nose** of your landsailer must move through the wind direction. In jibing, you move the stern through the wind direction as shown in Fig. 3-6.

Generally speaking, tacking consumes more time and speed than jibing. There are many times when tacking is necessary and unavoidable. Suppose you are sitting nose to wind, and wish to get a point directly ahead of you. The sail is luffing without pressure and the whole thing looks impossible. Not really. You will have to "tack" to get there. First head off at about 60 degrees in one direction for awhile (on one tack) then tack over "nose through the wind" so you are

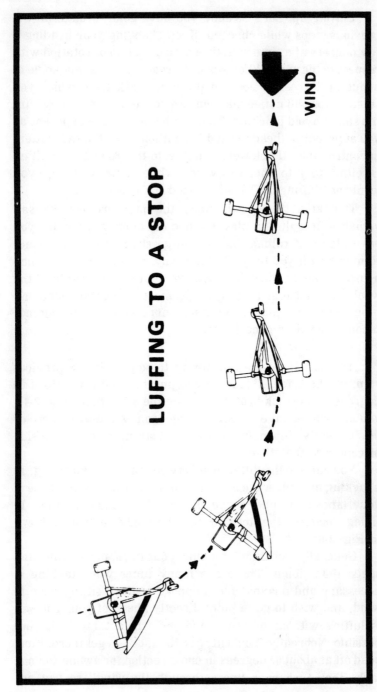

Fig. 3-3. The easiest way to stop is to turn into the wind and "luff."

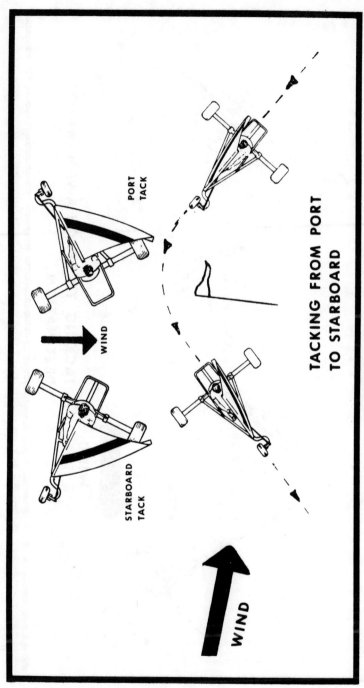

Fig. 3-4. Starboard and port tacks.

41

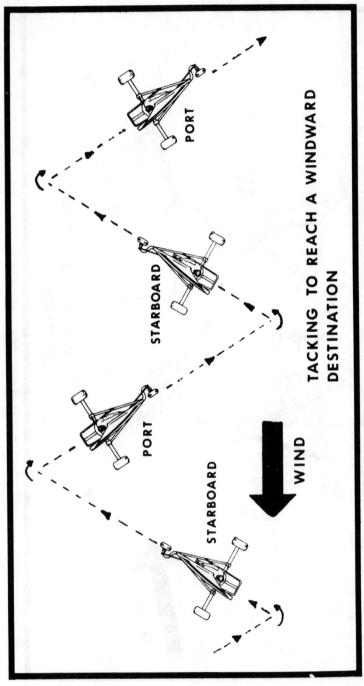

PORT

STARBOARD

PORT

STARBOARD

WIND

TACKING TO REACH A WINDWARD DESTINATION

Fig. 3-5. In order to sail into the wind, one must tack constantly.

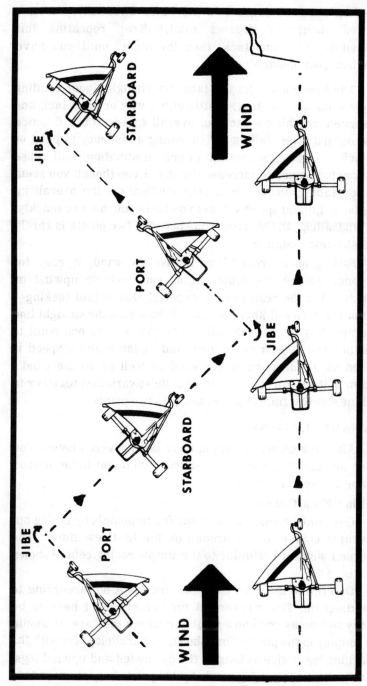

Fig. 3-6. Tacking downwind may be faster than running downwind.

heading about 60 degrees in the other direction (you have turned about 120 degrees total.) Keep repeating this procedure: first one tack, then the other, until you have reached your destination.

The Fine Points. As you tack, try changing your heading angle (and sail sheeting) a little either way on each tack and observe what this does to your overall speed. You will notice that often a little "falling off" (avoiding a tendency to point or "pinch" as close as possible to your destination) will cause your actual speed to increase greatly. Even though you seem to be heading further from your destination, the overall increase in ground speed will get you there much more quickly. In landsailing, the shortest **time** between two points is rarely the shortest distance.

Sailing on a "reach," or across the wind, is easy for anyone; getting the most out of your vehicle upwind or downwind is the realm of the experts! Downwimd tacking— actually a series of jibes back and forth across the straight line course—may be a much faster way to get from one point to another point, even dead downwind. A landsailer's speed is based on its direction to the wind as well as on the wind's strength itself. An expert puts all of these variables together to get the shortest time of travel between two points.

DYNAMIC LESSONS

All of the basics of sailing have been covered before you have actually "cast off" and sailed. You ought to be in good shape for your first sail!

Setting Up a Course

Get some practice in all of the fundamentals by laying out a simple course to sail around on the first few times. The course I suggest is similar to the simple racing course shown in Fig. 3-7.

Determine the wind direction and set it out according to the diagram. The markers at the corners don't have to be fancy so long as you know what and where they are. It should be roughly in the proportions shown—a parallelogram with the reaching legs twice as long as the downwind and upwind legs. A minimum area of 200 yards by 100 yards is recommended;

just be sure to allow plenty of room for luffing to a stop at the finish.

Preliminaries

With a light breeze blowing—say 8 to 12 knots—roll your fully rigged landsailer up to the starting pin of the course luffing head to wind. Hop into the seat, snap on seatbelt and goggles, and perhaps a pair of gloves. Grab the sheet in your left hand and place your feet on the steering bar. And relax!

Next, roll your vehicle around the starting line using your heels (or a push by a friend) and aim it toward the first mark of the course, holding yourself back with the hand brake or heels dug in.

The first leg is set up to be a reaching leg on the starboard tack. Using the sheet, trim the sail in until the boom is at an angle of roughly 45 degrees to the direction of the machine. As you trim it, you should feel a strain to take off. So do it! Steer for mark 1.

As your speed increases, watch the luff of your sail next to the mast, bringing the sheet in just quickly and smoothly enough to get rid of any bubble or flutter at the luff. **Don't overtrim!** If you think you have overtrimmed, don't hesitate to ease the sheet out until the luff flutters again and then trim slightly and smoothly back into the well trimmed position.

Experiment with trim until you have the hang of it. In general, as you speed up, you will be bringing the sheet in because the **apparent** wind will be moving forward. If you begin to slow down, the same apparent wind decreases and moves aft, so ease the sheet out as speed decreases. Overcome that natural tendency to pull it in tighter. Watch the luff of the sail and keep the flutter out.

This may seem like a lot to do in the first 200 yards but you can try it over and over again.

Approach the first mark a little "wide"—remember, you have a wide wheelbase under you so don't go around wiping out marks and other harmless spectators; it's poor style.

As you approach the first mark, begin to ease your sheet smoothly and steer widely around into the downwind leg of the course toward mark 2. Steer so that the **true** wind is exactly

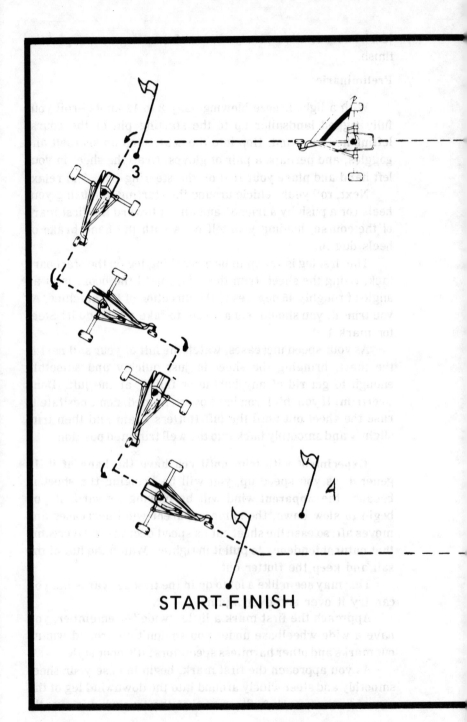

3

4

START-FINISH

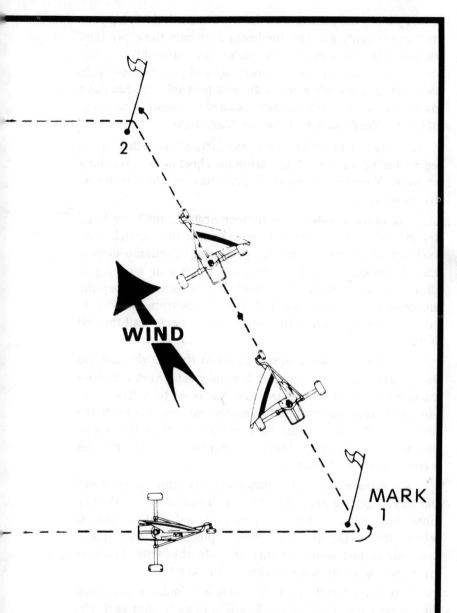

Fig. 3-7. A simple four corner race course can teach you all of the basic sailing maneuvers.

behind you. At the point where the wind is dead aft, bring your sheet in smoothly and jibe the boom over onto the other tack and ease the sheet out again quickly and smoothly. As the boom jibes, you may want to reach up and pull it across with one hand. If it doesn't want to go, you probably are not dead downwind: steer a little further "toward the boom" and it will snap over. Ease and head for mark 2, again taking it wide.

As you come around mark 2—the farthest from the start— begin steering for mark 3 and bring the sheet in for a reaching condition. Your speed should pick up. Play the sheet to see its effects on speed.

Take mark 3 wide. As you steer around, don't try to go straight for mark 4: you will have to **tack** on the fourth leg. As you head up toward the wind, keep sheeting in until the sheet is snug. In tacking "hard on the wind," use your steering to control the sail with the sheet held snug in. Steer to keep the bubble and flutter out of the luff. Steer away from the wind to increase your speed and then steer slowly back until the luff flutters.

When you can see mark 4, count to five slowly (not too slowly) and "kick" the steering to head you to mark 4 without changing the sheet. This puts you on the other tack. The boom will move over automatically and the sail will fill from the other side. Tacking should be a quick smooth action which changes your heading almost 120 degrees (less in heavier breezes, more in lighter.)

Concentrate more on maintaining good flow on your sail and less on getting around mark 4. You can always make two more short quick tacks at the mark to get around. This is better than stalling out from "pinching" too much. Landsailers just won't go directly into the wind, however much you tug on the sheet and kick your heels!

Take mark 4 on the port (left) side and continue on around the course a couple of times. It will get easier with each circuit. In three circuits or less, you really ought to have the hang of all the basic maneuvers: reaching, running, tacking and jibing, plus heading up, easing off, and rounding the marks on different points of sail.

Pointers

Some suggestions and things to observe while you sail around the course:

Experiment with sail trim and your direction of heading on each leg. You may begin to discover that falling off or heading up from the direct path between two marks gets you there faster (or slower) than the straight-line course. This could be particularly true on the downwind leg between 1 and 2: by holding off on a broader reach from the direct heading to 2 and then jibing swiftly over to a broad reach about halfway, you may get there more quickly than had you gone straight downwind and jibed.

Similarly in the wind or tacking leg, a little "reaching off"—which means you have to tack through a larger angle to the other tack—can really shorten the time between the two marks even though you have traveled considerably further over the ground. You can't reach off too far, however, for if you have to tack a full 180 degrees, you "can't get there from here." But for every wind speed there is an optimum tacking angle. Part of the art of landsailing is knowing relationships such as these.

Begin to use your ears as indicators too, in at least two ways. First, listen for the sound of your tires. This sound will tell you almost unconsciously a great deal about whether your speed is increasing or decreasing. Listen for the "pitch" of the hum as it increases or decreases with speed.

Also, listen for the difference in the ammount of hum between your windward and leeward wheel—especially on a reach. Your maximum speed generally occurs when the hum of the windward wheel (compared to the leeward) is the least. Uner this condition, the windward wheel is just barely touching the ground and its friction is at or near a minimum. You will learn when the wheel leaves the ground without looking at it, just from the sound.

Your ears are also excellent apparent-wind indicators. If you learn to sense the difference in airflow across them while you listen to the tire hum, you will soon be trimming "by ear," which frees your eyes for more useful tasks.

Plotting Angles

Choosing 12 to 18 knots as a good average, a chart of actual groundspeed-versus-heading-angle, with respect to the **true** wind direction, can be determined by trial and error. A typical chart is shown in Fig. 3-8. The angles around the chart give the direction to travel with respect to true wind direction: 0 degrees is directly upwind while 180 degrees is directly downwind. The circles labeled 1, 2, and 3 are relative groundspeed circles. If you multiply the relative speed on the chart by the actual wind speed of the moment, you obtain the actual groundspeed of the landsailer to be expected at that angle of heading. The curve is drawn for only one tack—it's the same for both sides.

Notice how steeply the curve increases between, say, the 50-degree heading and the 90-degree heading. Below 50 degrees, groundspeed goes to zero as you are pointed too high to the wind. Notice next how steeply the curve decreases between 90 degrees and 180 degrees. Dead downwind at 180 degrees, the speed is only about 90 percent of windspeed; dead downwind you can't go faster than the wind itself.

To determine the best heading angle to get from one point to another requires a few calculations. Taking the upwind case first, the optimum course (referred to as VMG, for "velocity made good") has been determined at a series of heading angles from 50 degrees to 90 degrees (above 90 degrees, of course, you are not making any progress toward your destination!).

These results are drawn into the graph in Fig. 3-9. The high point of the curve is the maximum VMG and occurs at a heading angle of just 65 degrees. At this angle, groundspeed is 150 percent of the true wind velocity and 100 percent higher than it would be if you were pinching up at 50 degrees. Tacking along the 65-degree heading angles will get you to a windward destination about 25 percent faster than a landsailer pinching along at 50 degrees. REMEMBER, you must tack through a total angle of 130 degrees (twice the 65-degree basic angle).

On the downwind leg, a similar set of calculations can be made resulting in the graph in Fig 3-10. This shows that the best VMG occurs at a heading of about 140 degrees with

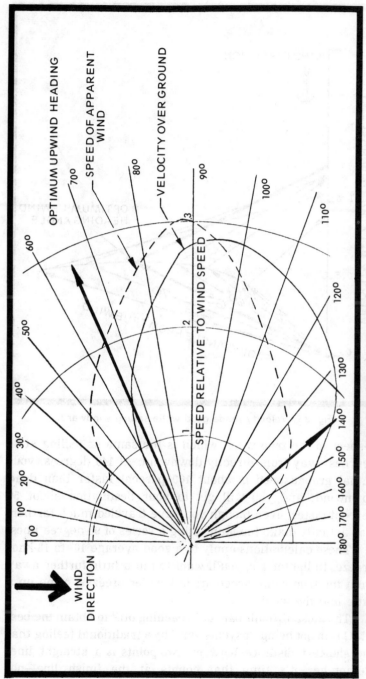

Fig. 3-8. Landsailer speed versus true wind speed.

OPTIMUM UPWIND HEADING

SPEED OF APPARENT WIND

VELOCITY OVER GROUND

WIND DIRECTION

SPEED RELATIVE TO WIND SPEED

0° 10° 20° 30° 40° 50° 60° 70° 80° 90° 100° 110° 120° 130° 140° 150° 160° 170° 180°

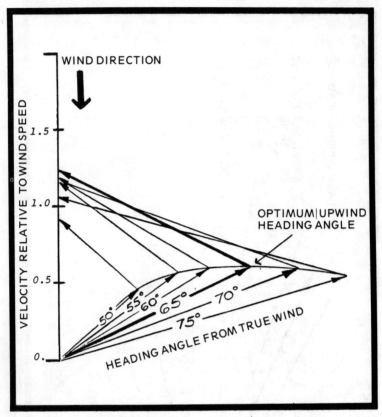

Fig. 3-9. Velocity made good while sailing windward.

respect to the true wind, which is the same as sailing at 40 degrees away from directly downwind. At 140 degrees, your actual groundspeed is about 100 percent faster than dead downwind; and you will get to your destination about 50 percent faster, even though you have traveled much farther. You actually make the jaunt using a series of 90-degree jibes.

These calculations apply to a good average 10- to 18-knot breeze. In lighter air, you'll want to fall a little further away from the true wind direction; in heavier breezes, come up a little into the wind.

The most difficult part of "reaching off" to obtain the best VMG is in not being "psyched out" by a traditional feeling that the shortest distance between two points is a straight line. Remember it's time that counts at the finish line—not distance! Just as difficult to overcome is the fear that a competitor who is pinching higher or going straight downwind will get there first—it may even look that way in the beginning. But when you shoot across ahead of him at about twice his speed, you'll be glad you had the courage of your convictions.

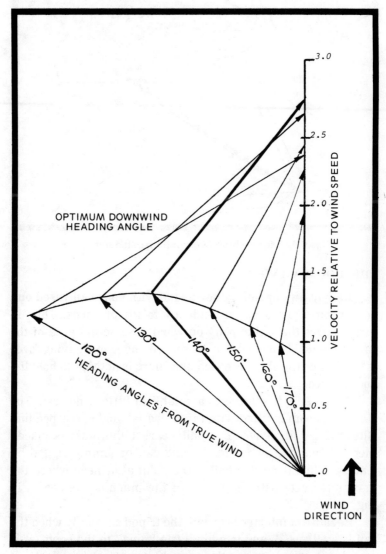

Fig. 3-10. Velocity made good while sailing downwind.

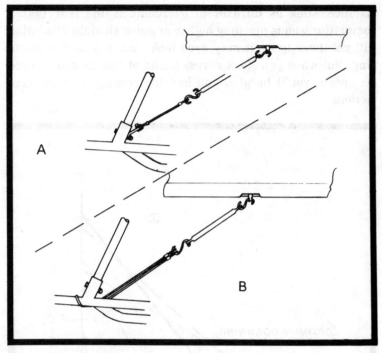

Fig. 3-11. A simple boom vang optimizes the sail shape.

THE BOOM VANG

In light airs or sailing downwind with your sail eased out, your boom always has a tendency to lift upwards. This, in turn, causes the sail to belly outward. The actual area of the sail presented to the wind is decreased and some driving force is lost. Since the sheet is eased out, there is nothing to hold the boom down.

A very simple solution is available at little or no cost. The standard boom is fitted with three "bails" and corresponding slits in the sail sleeve. The bail nearest the mast is placed there for vang attachment. A vang can be simply rigged by leading a line from this bail to the point at or near where the mast intersects with the frame of the machine, as shown in Fig. 3-11.

Because of interference with the tripod assembly when the sail is well eased, and to add a little "give" to the boom, it is worthwhile to place a rubber snubbing strap (available at

most hardware stores) in the vang. To attach it to the frame, a couple of alternatives are available. The mast retention bolt can be fitted with a strap with an eye or hole in it as in Fig. 3-11A. A single piece of line is then led to the snubbing strap and then to the bail. Even simpler, if less elegant, a piece of line can be worked under and over the frame as shown in Fig. 3-11B. The latter requires one less piece of hardware and can be rigged in seconds without the aid of any tools.

An added and possibly major advantage the vang can have is in preventing a "Chinese" or "goosewing" jibe—the

kind in which the boom and lower half of the sail go one way and the upper section of the sail goes the other. Who needs or wants broken battens, torn sails, or obvious indignity?

In using the vang, it should be slackened slightly in light airs to allow the boom to go out more easily. In heavy airs where there is plenty of wind pressure on the sail, the vang can be fairly snug.

SAFETY

As with any sport, landsailing can be hazardous unless certain safety rules are followed. Figure 3-12 includes a few hard-and-fast rules as well as suggestions for improving your enjoyment of landsailing.

BASIC RULES

1. For your own protection always wear a seatbelt.

2. For your own protection always wear goggles or eye protection.

3. Always choose a large area for sailing. Avoid collisions with natural or man-made obstacles as well as your fellow landsailors.

4. A landsailer is capable of high speeds and there is no adequate braking system for a swiftly moving vehicle. The front wheel brake is for parking only. Always operate a landsailer with caution allowing sufficient stopping distances to insure your own safety as well as that of other persons in the area.

GOOD SENSE

1. Learn the meaning of the basic words of landsailing.

2. Study the wind. Get a feel for things like direction, strength, variability. The wind is your fuel.

3. Study your sail. See what happens to its shape and direction as the wind blows on it. The sail is your powerplant.

4. Study your mainsheet, blocks and tackle and how they control the sail. The sheet is both your accelerator and brake.

5. Study your steering. Get a feel for which foot turns the landsailer in what direction and how much.

Fig. 3-12. Safety Rules

A WORD ABOUT SPEED

Under ideal conditions, a landsailer can reach speeds three times the speed of the wind. Landsailers have been clocked at over 70 mph. The very top speed would probably be near 100 mph. However, the helmsman can control the speed as he wishes by adjusting the sail position and direction of steering. A comfortable "cruising range" is between 20 mph and 50 mph which is within the normal prevailing wind range. You don't have to go any faster than you want to!

The Landsailer Market

While some avid landsailors prefer to build their own vehicles, the average sportsman would rather sail than build. To be sure, you must know a great deal about landsailing to be able to design a successful unit. In addition, you must be an expert craftsman (or have a lot of common sense and plenty of free advice available) plus a good supply of parts.

Imagine the plight of a man who wants to build a landsailer. He lives miles from a good-sized town, and he has never seen a commercially made unit. In fact, he may have only a vague idea of what he wants to do. Even if he gets hold of a catalog listing various sizes of steel tubes, fittings, etc., he will have a great deal of difficulty in deciding just what to buy. In addition, he will need specialized welding equipment, sewing machine for the sail, etc.

Clearly, the answer lies in purchasing a ready-made landsailer or at least a kit.

Recognizing the problems of home construction, several American manufacturers have sprung up and now, as a result, there are several good quality vehicles to choose from. They all have their advantages and disadvantages because they were designed with certain requirements in mind. Some feature low price, some feature good looks, and some feature top performance. A few try for everything.

It is somewhat characteristic of European landsailer designs that they are hard to transport, hard to assemble, and look more like contraptions. . .but they deliver superior performance! When matched against American-made landsailers on European soil and under European wind conditions, the European designs seem to always win. We must keep in mind that, in Europe, devotees of landsailing comprise quite a special group of individuals who are more performance-oriented than their U.S. counterparts. In the United States, design criteria such as medium price, easy transportability, good looks, and respectable performance are more important.

THE CHUBASCO STORY

Back in 1970, the young son of a California mechanical engineer wanted to build an 8-foot landsailer for himself. His father helped him engineer the vehicle and soon visualized exciting commercial potential in this sport. He obtained financing to set up production, became incorporated in 1971; today his firm is the largest landsailer manufacturer in the United States.

Frank Jayne, an affable, placid, yet highly competent engineer and businessman, kept good industrial design principles in mind during the development of his product. Having been a sailor since 1941, he had a rich background to draw from on sail design; yet, he realized that the speed at which landsailers run require extrapolation of orthodox water sailing techniques. Frank Jayne enlisted the help of Don Moyer to head up production efforts. When they first started up their company, landsailing was a tinkerer's field. Most vehicles were made from store-available fitting and pipes, but the sport was not gaining the popularity it warranted.

Looking for a suitable name for the new vehicle (Fig. 4-1), Frank and Don settled on **Chubasco**, which is the name of a hot Mexican wind. The prototype of Chubasco was full of fun and adventure. The designers wanted to achieve a pleasing look in their creation, yet it had to be rakish enough to look like it was doing 50 mph standing still. The seat cage, for instance, is not only a highly desirable safety feature but its chromed curve is designed to capture the imagination of today's speed-minded youth.

Let us now examine the Chubasco (Fig. 4-2) in detail. The main part of the chassis is a quasi-triangular structure, arc-welded from steel tubing. The stern of the unit (Fig. 4-3) is made from stainless steel. The rear axle and the mast is chrome and molybdenum. While most European designs support the mast in a swivel joint at its base and then "stay" it with guy wires, the Chubasco mast (Figs. 4-4 and 4-5) is held in

Fig. 4-1. The **Chubasco** is one of the most popular landsailers.

Fig. 4-2. The framework of the **Chubasco** is made entirely from steel to withstand the tremendous stresses.

Fig. 4-3. Assembling the **Chubasco** is simple. Rear axle is held to the chassis with two bolts.

Fig. 4-4. The steel mast is anchored to the chassis and supported by a sturdy triangulated frame.

two sockets at its bottom so that cumbersome assembly procedures are eliminated. In addition, the steel mast also becomes a very effective rollbar in case of a tipover. The sail is sewn by skilled sailmakers using 6 ounce **Dacron** material.

The finished dimensions are as follows: Overall length is 12 ft and height is almost 18 ft. The wheelbase is 7 ft. The weight (without driver) is about 200 lb, and the vehicle has a total sail area of 55 sq ft.

The driver sits in a contoured, **Naugahyde** bucket seat provided with a seatbelt. The pneumatic all-purpose tires are 18 inches in diameter in the front and 16 inches in the rear. The front wheel, equipped with a parking brake, is steered by a simple crossbar-pushrod arrangement, as shown in the photo of Fig. 4-6. The color scheme is picturesque: yellow chassis tubes, white sail with wide red stripe.

Following the practice of sailboats, each sail in the Chubasco class has a racing (serial) number on it.

With easy availability, good styling, and good performance, it is no wonder that the Chubasco is to American landsailing what the "MG" was to the sportscar scene back in the 1950s. The Chubasco can be transported atop a car.

Fig. 4-5. The last step in assembling the **Chubasco** is mounting the sail.

Fig. 4-6. A simple footpedal and pushrod steer the front wheel.

Assembly takes the average person about 10 minutes. Factory personnel have set an alltime record for assembling a Chubasco in less than 3 minutes.

"One-seater" Chubascos can be purchased as a complete vehicle (shipped in cartons) for $550. A more austere version, the **Dust Devil**, is in kit form but with all welding done. This model has no brakes and no seat cover, which brings the cost down to $450. The **Wind Animal** model is basically the same as the Chubasco but only the plans, assembly instructions, racing numbers, and sail emblem are available; the cost: $20.

An iceboat conversion kit is available to convert Chubascos for winter use. The price is $195. Speeds of up to 80 mph are possible. If you wish to try sailing on hard-packed snow, a set of three snowmobile runners can be snapped over the ice skates.

Chubascos are sold by the Lighthouse Landsailer Corp. 17865 Skypark Circle, Unit 18, Irvine Calif. 92707.

HONKER LANDSAILERS

The **Honker** landsailer (Fig. 4-7) is in a class by itself. Supporting 30-43 ft of sail, and weighing about 70 lb in racing

Fig. 4-7. The **Honker** landsailer is small but capable of high speeds.

Fig. 4-8. The framework is a triangle. The unit pictured in "parked"; when the driver is not in the cockpit, the **Honker** is up-ended to prevent it from being blown away.

trim, it is among the smallest and easiest-to-manage vehicles available.

Designed by Dick Dodd, the Honker is a study in simplicity. The basic frame of this unit(Fig. 4-8) is comprised of extruded aluminum tubes which are simply bolted together into a triangulated frame. The front and rear axles are made from steel. The mast is a reinforced aluminum tube, which breaks down into 6 ft sections for easy transportability. The sail is made from reinforced polyvinyl material and is fully battened. Steering, as shown in the photos of Figs. 4-9 and 4-10, is by front-wheel swiveling, which is controlled by a rubber-tipped crossbar located at the driver's feet. In the upper corner of Fig. 4-11, you can see the fitting foam-lined bucket seat and its seatbelt.

The Honker is shipped to you in two large cartons. The assembly procedure is simplicity itself: Using bolts and nuts only, the entire thing goes together in a few minutes. The nuts have nylon inserts that keep them locked in place. Add a little bit of grease to the wheel bearings, snug them up just so, and you will never again have to tinker with the chassis.

Fig. 4-9. The steering assembly is simplicity itself.

Fig. 4-10. A "direct-driven" foot bar controls front-wheel steering.

Fig. 4-11. The form-fitting seat sits over the chassis crossbar, the unit's center of gravity.

The mast is taken off the chassis and the sail is furled up when you transport the Honker, but the entire unit (Fig. 4-12) can be carried in a regular American-made sedan trunk. To be sure, the trunk lid will have to be left open and secured with a rope; however, the Honker will not protude out far enough to obstruct rear vision or to require a red flag. The beauty of this unit is precisely in its size and the ease with which you can handle it. It can be sailed even on a school yard or parking lot. Its top speed is a safe 35 mph or so, depending on your skill and the area of the sail.

The dimensions of the Honker are best stated in inches rather than feet. Length: 84 inches; width: 67 inches; height: 172 inches; sail: up to 43 sq ft. The unit weighs 65 lb.

Due to the size and construction of the Honker it is most suitable for sailing with a teenager or woman on board. While it will fully support a male adult, you will find that the boom is placed quite low and may hit your head as it swings around.

Also, performance-minded males may find the relatively small sail area insufficient to keep up with the larger land-sailers. Nevertheless, the Honker is an excellent "fun" vehicle. The price is low, from $199 up to $299, complete.

Accessories are available to make the Honker even better: Dacron sail, sail cover, racing numbers, anodized aluminum frame (racing red and dynamic blue), dual plastic-covered seats, belly pan, car-top carrier, airhorn, and ditty bag. An ice-sailing kit is also available for $150.

The story of the Honker does not end on land or ice. The latest addition to the product line: three molded hulls that transform your landsailer into a watersailer, thereby increasing its fun potential.

The hulls are completely enclosed catamaran-like pontoons which mount in place of the wheels. The weight of the craft increases to 120 lb empty, but two passengers can be carried on board.

For those who simply cannot afford a fully assembled landsailer but have some mechanical aptitude, Dick Dodd offers a set of blueprints for a vehicle called the **Rickshaw**. This unit is powered by a 33 sq ft sail and uses wheels from Stingray bikes.

Construction materials have been chosen from available general-hardware stock. Welding and drilling is required, and there are no step-by-step instructions, but the plans are drawn in such a way that one can easily visualize how the parts fit together. The seat for the driver is a stretched piece of canvas, sufficient to support a smallfish driver. Plans are available for $5 per set.

Honker Landsailers are located at 817 West Seventeenth Street, Costa Mesa, Calif. 92627.

THE WINDBUGGY

Windbuggy Mfg. Co. is another manufacturer of parts and complete landsailers. Their mailing address is: Westminster Ave., Newport Beach, Calif. 92660. The flagship of their fleet (Fig. 4-14) is the **Windbuggy Competition Class II**, a model which carries 109 sq ft of sail on an extruded-aluminum, top-stayed mast.

The main advantage of this model is in its light weight: 133 lb fully rigged. This means (1) that you can easily carry it atop your car and (2) that it can be sailed on soft ground without wheel-sinking. For heavier winds, one can

Fig. 4-12. The Hornet can share a car top with a boat.

always add more ballast in the form of an extra passenger. The brake is the quick-release European-type racing lever. The chassis is made from steel tubes. The cockpit (seat) is a simple canvas affair to save weight. The rear axle can be disassembled to a mere 3 tubes (for transportation), yet it can be telescoped out to 8, 10, or even 12 ft, depending on wind conditions.

Fully finished, the whole vehicle represents an investment of $500. The company sells complete plans for $40 to anyone wishing to "roll his own."

The **Windbuggy Junior** (Fig. 4-15) is an extremely clean and sturdy little vehicle intended mainly for children. It carries 40 sq ft of flat sail. To simplify things, there is no boom and there are no battens. The mast is a unique "unsupported luff spar" and the sail can be simply rolled up around it when not in use or in high winds. The chassis (Fig. 4-16) is made from heavy plywood cut to a rough triangular shape and varnished. There is room for two children or one adult on this rig.

Completely finished, the vehicle (Fig. 4-17) sells for about $275. Plans are also available for $20 per complete set. Parts

Fig. 4-13. The **Honker** can also be adapted to water use by the addition of three pontoons which replace the wheels.

Fig. 4-14. The **Windbuggy** competition model.

Fig. 4-15. The **Windbuggy Junior** is an ideal vehicle for children.

Fig. 4-16. The chassis is heavy plywood. The framework bolts to the plywood, making a sturdy, rigid vehicle.

Fig. 4-17. The completely finished **Windbuggy Junior.**

for a "kit approach" can be purchased for about $100, and full kits for $150. Designer Don Rypinski hopes the price will be further reduced when good quality plastic sails become available.

The **Windbuggy Junior** actually started out as a design aimed at providing handicapped children with a safe and educational recreation activity in Anaheim, California. The city even offers a low-cost course in landsailing for any interested child. The photo of Fig. 4-18 shows one of the classes in progress.

FENIX INTERNATIONAL SAILER

For those who are willing to pay for top performance and good looks, there is a fantastic vehicle, available from Holland, called the **Fenix.** Carrying 109 sq ft of sail and piloted by its designer Hans Dekkers of Holland, the prototype of this vehicle was European champion for four straight years and World Champion in 1970. It sports a molded fiber-glass body which extends from the gigantic wingmast to well behind the rear axle. Three Citroen automobile wheels carry the full 550 lb weight of this unit. The price of the complete sailer, $1750, makes this the Rolls Royce of the landsailers.

The pilot has a fully instrumented cockpit in which two automobile steering wheels are installed: one is connected to the front wheel steering while the other handles the sails. In light airs (5 mph wind) the Fenix can sail five times faster than the speed of the wind, while in strong winds the speeds may be well over 70 mph. A passenger may also be carried in the cockpit.

"DN" CLASS LANDSAILERS

There is no doubt that the most popular iceboat in the world is the DN class. (See a complete description in the chapter on iceboating.) Designed primarily as an iceboat, it nevertheless lends itself to conversion for snow skis or wheels. The first wheeled DN appeared around 1964 mainly in Europe. Sporting a sail of up to 79 sq ft, it has full-length battens, a center grooved mast made from wood, a wooden "plank" (which carries the outrigger rear wheels), and a body which bears a slight resemblance to a duckboat. This land yacht is a dandy little unit which lends itself admirably to home construction. Plans are available for as little as 60 cents. Hardware is also

Fig. 4-18. Anaheim's Park and Recreation Department gives class in landsailing.

available from various sources, but there is a full-time manufacturer from whom one can order any or all of the hardware: W. Sarns Mfg., 38101 Huron Point Drive, Mt. Clemens, Mich. 48043. A sail costs $105. Wood parts can be made in any home workshop for less than $100. The unit can be taken apart for easy transport on your car top.

In competitions the DN class is very closely controlled. Most parts of this sailer must conform to a specific design configuration and no deviations are accepted. This is required in order that the competition may be very keen and so that the results will reflect the pilot's ability rather than the status of his bank balance.

The North American Land Sailing Association has DN plans available for its members at a very nominal cost. The plans are in the form of a huge blueprint, with basic construction and assembly instructions written on the side of the print.

SAND SAILER AND DESERT DART

Special mention must be made here of the two landsailers originally developed by John Schindler, one of the true giants and pioneers of landsailing in the United States. John developed his **Sand Sailer** (Fig. 4-19) in 1962 and originally sold it fully assembled and in kit form. As more and more people got to know the sport of landsailing, a steady demand developed for plans. At this time, no fully assembled kit form Sand Sailers are available but you can order a $2.50 set of plans: a large sheet on which several drawings appear to illustrate the overall layout as well as design details of every part. There is also a list of materials. The plans for Sand Sailer are sold by **NuSport**, 5221 Rockland Ave, Los Angeles, Calif. 90041. (Telephone 213-256-0705).

The Sand Sailer has a 45 sq-ft/sail on an unstayed mast. The chassis is made from steel tubing, electrically welded. Wheels are of the light-duty "drop center" type. You may even be able to use rubber tired wheelbarrow wheels if you are careful to select a type that will withstand heavy sideloads. The vehicle weighs about 120 pounds fully built. NuSport also has plans for another vehicle, called **Desert Dart** (Fig. 4-20),

Fig. 4-19. **SandSailer, developed** by Schindler.

Fig. 4-20. The **Desert Dart**, designed by Schindler, was the first landsailer in the U.S. to use a raked mast.

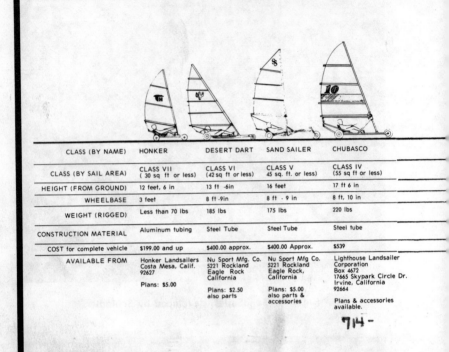

CLASS (BY NAME)	HONKER	DESERT DART	SAND SAILER	CHUBASCO
CLASS (BY SAIL AREA)	CLASS VII (30 sq ft or less)	CLASS VI (42 sq ft or less)	CLASS V 45 sq. ft. or less)	CLASS IV (55 sq ft or less)
HEIGHT (FROM GROUND)	12 feet, 6 in	13 ft -6in	16 feet	17 ft 6 in
WHEELBASE	3 feet	8 ft -9in	8 ft - 9 in	8 ft, 10 in
WEIGHT (RIGGED)	Less than 70 lbs	185 lbs	175 lbs	220 lbs
CONSTRUCTION MATERIAL	Aluminum tubing	Steel Tube	Steel Tube	Steel tube
COST for complete vehicle	$199.00 and up	$400.00 approx.	$400.00 Approx.	$539
AVAILABLE FROM	Honker Landsailers Costa Mesa, Calif. 92627 Plans: $5.00	Nu Sport Mfg. Co. 5221 Rockland Eagle Rock California Plans: $2.50 also parts	Nu Sport Mfg Co. 5221 Rockland Eagle Rock, California Plans: $5.00 also parts & accessories	Lighthouse Landsailer Corporation Box 4672 17665 Skypark Circle Dr. Irvine, California 92664 Plans & accessories available.

714 -

which carries 41 sq ft of sail. This was the first landsailer in the United States with a raked mast. It is extremely fast to windward. The chassis is topped with a very pretty looking molded body which is available on special order only. While the Desert Dart at one time sold for $420, it is no longer available assembled.

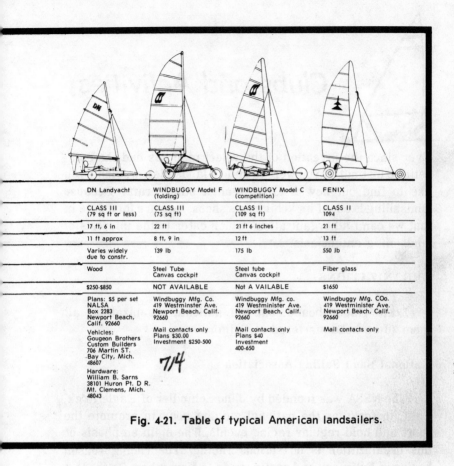

	DN Landyacht	WINDBUGGY Model F (folding)	WINDBUGGY Model C (competition)	FENIX
	CLASS III (79 sq ft or less)	CLASS III (75 sq ft)	CLASS II (109 sq ft)	CLASS II 1094
	17 ft, 6 in	22 ft	21 ft 6 inches	21 ft
	11 ft approx	8 ft, 9 in	12 ft	13 ft
	Varies widely due to constr.	139 lb	175 lb	550 lb
	Wood	Steel Tube Canvas cockpit	Steel tube Canvas cockpit	Fiber glass
	$250-$850	NOT AVAILABLE	Not A VAILABLE	$1650
	Plans: $5 per set NALSA Box 2283 Newport Beach, Calif. 92660	Windbuggy Mfg. Co. 419 Westminster Ave. Newport Beach, Calif. 92660	Windbuggy Mfg. co. 419 Westminister Ave. Newport Beach, Calif. 92660	Windbuggy Mfg. COo. 419 Westminster Ave. Newport Beach, Calif. 92660
	Vehicles: Gougeon Brothers Custom Builders 706 Martin ST. Bay City, Mich. 48607	Mail contacts only Plans $30.00 Investment $250-500	Mail contacts only Plans $40 Investment 400-650	Mail contacts only
	Hardware: William B. Sarns 38101 Huron Pt. D R. Mt. Clemens, Mich. 48043			

Fig. 4-21. Table of typical American landsailers.

Comparison of Specs

The two-page spread of Fig. 4-21 shows the basic characteristics of typical American landsailers. At the top of each column is a sketch of the vehicle in that class.

5   *Clubs and Activities*

Ever since the invention of the wheel man has had the competitive instinct. If you were to build a landsailer, wouldn't you like to find out how it fares against other craft? Because landsailing is out of its "children's shoes," we are fortunate in that we can find organizations which cater to the interests of landsailing enthusiasts.

ORGANIZATIONS

Local clubs abound, but the **national** organizations all seem to be headquartered in California.

National Sand Sailing Association

The NSSA was founded by John Schindler of Eagle Rock, Calif. to serve as the national guiding body to promote the sport and hold regular racing events. The main emphasis of this organization is on serious racing. The racing season begins in February and continues on to November. On the last Saturday of the racing season, the organization holds a trophy banquet to award prizes to the winners of the **Open, Women's and Junior** divisions. The members usually camp right at the race course, located on a dry lake in the Mojave Desert, about 100 miles from Los Angeles on the road to Las Vegas.

A number of NSSA members have competed successfully in the world championship regatta in England against experts from all over the globe.

Outside of the active race program the advantages of belonging to the organization include a monthly newsletter as well as lowered prices on racing equipment such as helmets, tools, goggles, and parts. A self-addressed stamped envelope mailed to NSSA, 7305 Van Nuys Blvd., Vans Nuys, Calif. 91405

will bring you information about landsailing and the
organization.

North American Land Sailing Association

A California landsailing pioneer, Don Rypinski, founded
the North American Land Sailing Association in 1969. This is
the U.S. affiliate of the international FISLY (Europe)
governing body for international landsailing. They are a
highly sophisticated racing group, placing great emphasis on
the technical and international aspects of the sport. They
welcome newcomers interested in any aspect of the sport, and
cite as their specific objectives: to develop an exciting, safe,
nonpolluting form of recreation into a nationally recognized
sport; to disseminate, by means of a bimonthly journal, ideas
on landsailing design, research, activites, etc.); to assist in
making available vehicles for rent, lease, or sale; to collect
and distribute information about landsailers; to assist
members in locating suitable sailing areas; to provide racing
rules; to provide insurance against property damage and
personal injury; to arrange U.S. representation in international contests (and host a world championship event in
the USA).

Annual membership fees for active members is $10, which
includes insurance plus a subscription to the bimonthly
publication. The racing rules are available separately for
$2.50.

It is the ultimate aim of NALSA to serve as the main
governing body for landsailing in the United States. While they
help new groups to get started, their main purpose is to serve
as a clearinghouse for information and as a sort of a catalyst
for landsailing activities in general. They are not actively
interested in getting local groups started; rather, they would
like any and all local groups to govern themselves and to affiliate with NALSA (there is no charge for this) so that right
from the start the new group will be racing under the well
established international rules which have been tried and
tested throughout the years. In this way, it is hoped,
classification of yachts and race procedures will be uniform.
As of this writing, members of NALSA have just returned

from Europe where they have been participating in the world championships and the second trans-Sahara land-yacht expedition. Thus, they are in close contact with pilots and organizations from all over the world.

Local groups usually find that there is only one objection raised by owners of sites suitable for landsailing: the group must have liability insurance. Here again, if you need to acquire liability insurance, NALSA can help because they have the longest history on file with major U.S. insurance companies.

If you care to find out all about this interesting organization, send a self-addressed stamped envelope to: NALSA, Box 2283, Newport Beach, Calif. 92660.

American Land Sailing Organization

This is the third, and perhaps the largest group of sailers, and is sponsored by the Lighthouse Landsailers company. Their purposes are entirely unselfish, as they wish to promote landsailing in general, with particular interest in one-design activities for the owners of **Chubasco** landsailers.

The primary tasks of ALSO are to organize and manage landsailing events for its members, supervise one-design class standards and measurement functions; to provide a communications link between Chubasco owners; and to locate and publicize areas suitable for landsailing.

Meetings are informal. Members are encouraged to bring and show movies and slides, discuss their latest developments, and to generally chit-chat and have a grand old time. The emphasis is on "having fun with your landsailer" rather than on detailed technical arguments of racing rules.

Each member receives a membership card, a jacket patch, a subscription to a monthly newsletter, a copy of the bylaws and racing rules, and a discount on various products. All members, of course, are eligible to compete in club-sponsored racing events. Their racing classes are **Open, Junior, Women, Senior B, and Senior A.** They are even considering a handicapping system to equalize some of the differences between various rigs and specialized equipment. A postcard addressed to ALSO, Box 4652, Irvine, Calif. 92664 will bring you a host of literature and information.

ACTIVITIES

What is it like to go out to a club race? To begin with, you will find a large open area (beach, dry lake, parking lot, abandoned airfield, etc.) and a large number of people. There is a welcome absence of earsplitting noise and noxious fumes. Here and there the "pilots" are assembling or tuning their landsailers, while members of their families either pitch in or tend to other chores such as setting up a tent, preparing food or serving drinks. In the background, you'll see street vehicles of every type parked and set up for "ground support."

The atmosphere is friendly and relaxed. You do not find more than friendly rivalry here, as equipment performance is deemed secondary to sailing ability and experience. Here and there you hear the familiar pop of an opening beer can or soft-drink bottle. A guitar may be strumming softly and kids are playing.

Then...suddenly...the breeze becomes a brisk wind! Sails stiffen, here and there a driverless vehicle begins to move and several hands hastily grab for it. "Wind is up" is the cry, and landsailors jump into their vehicles and strap themselves in. In a flash, they're off for the far end of the runway, dispersed and flying. When it is certain that this indeed is a lasting wind, racing soon begins.

The above may be a typical picture of a "landsailing meet" in California, where inland breezes do not pick up until about noon. Near beaches or open areas far from the ocean there may be a more or less constant wind blowing, or at least regularly repeating cycles of wind gusting.

ACTIVITIES IN EUROPE

The sport of landsailing began in Europe; for this reason, it has developed to a higher degree of proficiency there than in the U.S.A. While U.S. landsailors are mostly unorganized sportsmen out for fun, our European counterparts are highly

Fig. 5-1. The entire family can enjoy landsailing...one at a time or all together. The street vehicles parked alongside the course are set up for such support activities as camping and picnicking.

organized. Their vehicles reflect a higher degree of sophistication. A conservative estimate may place the number of European "pilots" at more than 2000 and their number is growing fast. Let us look at the typical profile of a pilot in each country.

Fig. 5-2. Club get-togethers can be relaxed or fiercely competitive. Here a group of **Chubascos** feel the first gust.

Fig. 5-3. A brief flurry of wind and the desert is dotted with sails. Here, the "yachts" are **Sandsailers.**

France

In France they call the land yacht, "le char a voile" (vehicle of wind). Most of the landsailors are quite young. Their carefree spirit and love of camaraderie suits them very well to this sport. The most famous group is centered around a monastery. Near the little town of Vernon, the local priest **L'abbe Pierre Marle** has organized many young boys in an orphanage into a tightly knit sailing group. His purpose in doing so was to "build character" through (1) encouraging a high degree of workmanship in building the vehicles, and (2) developing within the boys a fierce competitive spirit. One of the boys became world champion in 1969.

On any one weekend you may find as many as 800 boys sailing in France.

Germany

The German group is a well organized fraternity whose average age (as well as average income level) is higher than in the surrounding countries. Through the efforts of Helmut Spielman, they started making great strides in the early 1960s.

Most of their yachts are kept near the dikes by the ocean. During the great floods of 1971, a sudden tide threatened the land yachts with destruction and, out of sheer enthusiasm for the sport, the local townspeople rushed to the rescue in the middle of the night.

Germans call their vehicles "Strandsegler" (meaning beach sailers). They organize their races with thoroughness and go to great lengths to advertise upcoming events. The price of a German landsailer may be more than $3000 (which may not seem so high considering the fact that most of their pilots drive Mercedes cars). The sails of the German yachts carry a large "G" for Germany.

Belgium

When you see a sail with a large "B" on it, you know that it hails from Belgium. The average Belgian landsailor is a common, everyday man who loves the wind and speed. He may be young or old and he always races his yacht along the coast where, at low tide, the beach may be very wide. The president of the Federation Internationale de Sand and Land Yachts lives in Belgium. Belgium even has a special beach, 12 miles long, reserved for landsailing. There is a club house at each end of the course.

Denmark

Denmark is just beginning to get involved in land yachting. One of the original members, Leif Moller, had built himself a sail powered vehicle in 1959 and thought that he had actually invented a new sport. One day, sailing along the beach, he came upon an interested spectator, a German tourist, who enlightened Herr Moller and explained that this was a very old sport indeed.

England

Across the channel, you will find the British enthusiast racing his vehicle on old abandoned RAF airfields. The British like to build their own landsailers and we can find examples of great engineering skill as well as craftsmanship here. Following the practices in high-performance racecar construction, these vehicles have space frames welded from bits and pieces of steel tubing. The sails, steering gears, suspension and braking mechanisms are mostly of original design. One English vehicle could be steered to go in any direction including sideways. It as thus possible to run the car in any direction while maintaining the sail at an optimum and constant angle to the wind. The pilot assumed a prone position and had to operate several levers and steering wheel.

The European Vehicle

If you were to look at pictures of a typical U.S. race and compare it with pictures taken at the last European championships you would notice that American land yachts are equipped with smallish wheels, have open cockpits and spindly masts. In contrast, the European yachts have automobile wheels and tires, fully enclosed bodies, and wide masts which act as leading edges for the superefficient airfoil-like sails. The body of the yacht, made from fiber glass or aluminum, may resemble a dirt-track dragster or iceboat.

The masts are usually "stayed" with wires, which means that the bottom of the mast swivels in a pivot (so that it can rotate as the sail is adjusted to the optimum angle). The top of the mast is tethered to the body and axles of the yacht by means of steel cables.

The rear wheels have a very wide track. The rear axle is supported by a wooden cross member whose purpose is to provide springing without the use of springs.

There are quite a few Class I sailers around at every race. These are the huge, fast, exciting yachts that may cost up to $3000 and weigh as much as a ton. Their performance can be simply summed up as "awesome" as they race down the beaches.

The European Race Course

The average European race goes on for about 12 miles. The race course is usually laid out on the beach in 5 or 10 legs. Since the slope angle of the beach is shallow, whenever the tide comes in the water advances tremendously fast along the beach. As a consequence, pilots often find themselves in a race with the tide as well as their rivals.

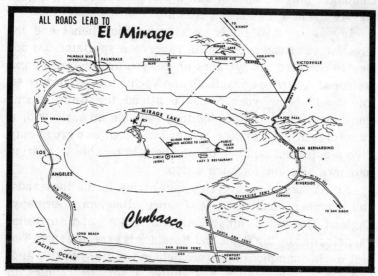

Fig. 5-4. A map showing the location of one of America's most popular sailing sites. About two hours from Los Angeles.

On the other hand, the receding tide may leave great puddles of water in the depressions of the beach and when the yachts hit these miniature lakes at 50 mph, the spray rides high! As a result of constant exposure to the salt spray, European landsailors wear full-length rainsuits. To protect themselves from the biting wind, they also wear gloves. Crash helmets are mandatory in view of the high speeds attained.

THE EUROPEAN RACE

European races are started with the pilots standing beside their yachts. At the drop of the flag they push their own vehicles without outside help. It is important to reach a fairly high speed before the pilot finally jumps into his seat and begins to sail. Many a race has been lost because the pilot jumped into his yacht too soon with the resulting loss of position. To facilitate this " le Mans" start, many yachts are equipped with a hand tiller so that they can be steered even when the yachtsman is not sitting.

While it is imperative in any racing situation to know the meaning of the signals and flags, it is especially important to be aware of flags in Europe where as many as six or eight languages may be spoken and a misunderstood flag signal may result in a high speed crash.

If you are a beginner, it is very educational and interesting to attend a European race, as a spectator. Do not plan to compete in any races unless you are thoroughly experienced. There are practically no yachts for rent or hire so you should bring your own. To attend the world championships, it is recommended that you sign up early with a travel club in order to get a low air fare. Your own group may have a sufficient number of members to be able to charter your own airplane for such a trip.

FISLY has a membership numbering in the thousands. The member countries are France, Belgium, Germany, England, Holland, Denmark, Algeria, U.S.A., and Australia. Participation by the Poles and Russians is expected soon. The first world championships were held in Germany in 1963 and, since then, the location has shifted from one country to another.

Fig. 5-5. There is nothing like enjoying your favorite sport in the company of others with similar interests.

Fig. 5-6. A typical European scene: the spray flies as the wing-masted **Fenix** flies down a shallow beach.

Fig. 5-7. Acquiring landsailing information and techniques is easy when you belong to a club.

Starting An Organization

No hobby or sport is completely satisfying unless one can share it with others of similar interests. When you are a land-sailor you want to be where the "language is spoken." If you are the first in your area to partake in this relatively new sport you should take it upon yourself to seek out potential enthusiasts and to organize a club.

But where do you find people with similar interests? This is not as difficult as it sounds. First, you can write to the various manufacturers of landsailers and ask them for names and addresses of people to whom they have sold their products in your area. Explain your purpose for wanting this information and they will be more than happy to help you out. You should also write to the editors of the national landsailing association newsletters and ask them to inform you in case somebody in your area has the same ideas as you do or, to put you in touch with others of like interest.

You can also attend local sports shows, recreational exhibits, and similar activities. You can make up a mimeographed circular which outlines your interest in forming a club and either display it on supermarket bulletin boards or send it to sports clubs, men's clubs, boating organizations, etc. Sketch a landsailer on the announcement and briefly describe what landsailing is all about so that even casually interested people will want to contact you.

If you own a movie camera, take action shots of land-sailing activities at one of the centers for this sport and, during the initial club meeting show this movie to further kindle interest.

The Meeting

The first meeting should outline your plans for forming a group and how you propose to go about it. While you are at it, elect a group of officers who will then be charged with organizing and running further activities. Make sure that there is a brochure available for free distribution to anyone attending the meeting. There are professionally made posters available (from commercial manufacturers) publicizing this sport.

Fig. 5-8. Sailing sites are often easy to obtain for official club use.

Try to invite owners of local sporting goods stores to your meeting and encourage them to stock landsailers and parts. It is imperative that there be a site and equipment available for anyone who wishes to see landsailers in action. If there is a vehicle available, ask the owner to demonstrate it and to arrange for demo rides.

Local radio stations, newspapers, and TV stations always seem interested in helping new groups get started. A short notice in any of these media can do wonders for your fledgling group.

Often, when somebody sees a landsailer in action (perhaps when driving by a sailing site and accidentally spotting it), he stops and asks questions. He may come back armed with his camera to take pictures for later viewing in his own hometown. He then becomes the emissary, even though he's had but a brief exposure to this sport.

It is interesting to note that several manufacturers are reporting great success with local dealers who are enthusiasts first and dealers second. Thus, instead of a disinterested commercial store, the newcomer to landsailing is helped along by an enthusiast who is more than willing to spend time instructing the novice. The result is a new friendship formed, more activity in the area, and another landsailer sold.

Duties of Officeholders

As an aid to clubs getting organized, here is a list of duties performed by the elected officers of an average organization.

President- Presides over official meetings. Guides and develops the club in accordance with the goals set down in the bylaws. Organizes, deputizes, and supervises. Represents the club at social functions, in front of civic groups, in communications media, and at other clubs.

Vice President- Substitutes for the president whenever necessary. Heads committees by appointment.

Secretary- Keeps a register of the members, keeps a record and minutes of meetings, general correspondence with individuals and outside clubs. Answers inquiries.

Treasurer-Holds the club funds, provides an accounting for them, and disburses checks whenever so instructed by the president. Makes financial reports at regular intervals.

Social chairman-Initiates functions of social nature, welcomes newcomers, organizes social events.

Liaison officer- Serves as publicity chairman; provides information about the club to outside media, negotiates with landowners for the use of sailing sites.

Editor-Gathers, types, and gets the club bulletin printed; mails to members and interested outsiders.

Racing

6

Ever since the second landsailer was built, there has existed a rivalry between pilots: which vehicle is faster? Similarly, whenever landsailors gather, friendly rivalry (or fierce competition) usually demands that a race be held.

A race may be quite informal or it may approach the seriousness of the Olympiad. You may be tacking upwind at the edge of your favorite parking lot when, suddenly, you realize that not quite 100 feet behind you there is another landsailer. You subconsciously tighten up on the sail and then take a "casual" look behind: "Am I leaving him behind or is he catching up?"

You may also spend weeks preparing your vehicle—and yourself—for that "best two out of three events" feature race that will determine the state champion.

Whatever your reason, knowing what to expect and how to prepare for it should be of some help to you.

SELECTION OF A SITE

Site selection is the first and most important aspect of organizing a good race. Nothing detracts from a race more than a poor track. What you should keep foremost in mind is this: the program should be tailored to the participants and their vehicles. There is no formal requirement for landsailing races that says you should have such and such a layout or length or size.

If your group has small yachts, with sails of 30-40 sq ft (such as commercially available **Honkers**), you may find that a minimum of 25,000 sq ft of space will suffice. If your group is quite advanced and there are some large yachts (such as a **Fenix**), you may need a mile or more of land at least.

The track itself should be either of square shape or, if it is narrow, it should be oriented so that the prevailing wind

Fig. 6-1. A group of DN class land yachts being pushed off to start a race.

blows across it from the side. A wind blowing along the length of a narrow track will blow all of the vehicles "down" but many will never be able to return under their own steam.

An area which has a width of at least five highway lanes is sufficient for the average land yacht to tack in a zigzag fashion. The wider the better, of course, to provide ample room for wheel-to-wheel duels by several pilots.

Abandoned airfields may be triangular in shape and thus provide a really great track where sailing upwind, downwind, and crosswind will be possible much like the triangular race courses laid out for sailboats.

The track should be accessible and well marked so that competitors will be able to find it easily. There should be basic "human comfort" facilities such as parking, toilets, drinking water, etc. Buildings or trees should not be located near the edge of the track because these will obstruct the wind, create turbulent eddies, and reduce visibility.

THE TRACK

You may mark the track layout by almost any method available to you. The most common is the use of colored flags or oil drums at the inside of each turn. The flags should have a bright color, such as orange. The flags, usually about 24 inches square, are fastened to the top of 6 ft poles.

You may develop your own flag color standards but it is best to adhere to international standards. For instance, in European racing they place an orange flag at the end of the straightaway near the entrance to the turn. This signifies an area in which it is forbidden to pass the leader until you are out of the turn and out of the orange zone.

PARTICULARS OF THE RACE

Entry fees should be kept low so that the "fun" aspect of the sport is maintained. Most clubs charge a fee of $1 per day, which covers all races entered by the competitor.

The starting line should be marked in some way or the competitors must be told that the imaginary line between two flags will serve as the line. About 30 minutes before the race it is customary to raise a white flag on a tall pole. This flag is located right at the starting line near the chief steward's "desk" where he keeps his paperwork.

A blue flag is raised five minutes before the race. The competitors then push their vehicles to the starting line and park it there with the front wheel pointing down the first leg of the course. If a formal pilots' meeting is to be held a green-yellow flag is raised. If no meeting is held it is still advisable to announce to the pilot (via a bullhorn or PA system) how many laps will be raced. This is always a welcome announcement because in the excitement of the race, many competitors forget such details.

The race is started by dropping a green flag. The competitors may be strapped into their seats and pushed by an assistant (the preferred U.S. method of starting) or the pilots themselves may push their vehicles and jump in when sufficient speed has been reached.

As the cars pass the starting line it is customary to call out their completed laps to them. It is also helpful to shout "one lap to go" at the appropriate time. When the cars cross the finish line, the starter honks a horn to signify their completing the race.

As your club grows you will find it helpful to issue a competitor's log card to every entrant. On this card, the chief steward should fill in the date, windspeed, course layout, laps, and place of finish. This card will then serve as a permanent record for each competitor and may be used in determining the season totals or for other purposes.

At the end of the season, the competitor may then ascertain if he is a light-wind or heavy-wind sailor, depending on the results attained under a variety of circumstances.

Prizes may be awarded, depending on the financial status of the club and the amount of entry fee charged. Ribbons or donated merchandise prizes are always welcomed by the pilots. Any tangible evidence of a sailor's achievement will bring him back for many more events.

THE PROGRAM

A typical local race program may go something like this:

First: Preparation, testing, lunch. (Wait until the wind comes up and reaches a reliable and predictable level of at least 10 mph.)

When Wind Permits:

Junior races

Ladies races

Open class any vehicles)

One-design (for one-make vehicles)

Over-30 pilots

Treasure hunt (at each flag there is a written instruction on where the next instruction will be found).

Follow the leader (the faster landsailer leads off, the others try to catch him).

There is virtually no end to the variety of races that can be held. If there are many vehicles you can repeat the same type of race several times. It is generally better to hold races to about two laps per heat but have more races. This creates more excitement than holding long-distance races which usually end up being a runaway for one lucky man-vehicle combination for that day. The more vehicles there are competing, the longer the course should be (and the higher the number of laps).

Now, a word about **one-design** and **unlimited** racing. One-design races are held for vehicles of the same manufacturer or made from the same plans. Only very small variations are permitted so as to keep the competition keen. These variations are clearly outlined by the club or by the body which controls one-design racing. In unlimited racing, all vehicles are allowed to compete in the same event regardless of size. Handicapping may be done, although as yet there has been no reliable formula developed other than subdividing by sail area only. Handicapping may be by recomputing the time of finish or by allowing the vehicles to start at predetermined intervals. You can eliminate "sandbagging" by automatically advancing the winner of a race into the next higher class. This may be a senior class or a class where larger sails are used.

At any rate, until your club develops a large number of experienced sailors, it is best to hold as many races as possible with all entrants lumped into one class. Eventually a pattern will develop and classifications will suggest themselves. If your club belongs to a national organization, their rules should be followed as soon as the general level of the proficiency and the number of competitors permit.

SAILING TIPS

You can learn almost as much from watching others sail as sailing yourself. For instance, at the recent Mile Square and Rancho California sail-ins, the course was small and the spectating was excellent. Why did the winners win and losers lose? Here are some observations.

Tacking Upwind

Winners take longer tacks and thereby less tacks—every tack costs some time and speed even when perfectly executed.

Losers wait until they have slowed considerably before they tack, not only losing time in the tack but momentum needed to keep up speed on the next tack.

Winners while on one tack are not only deciding early in this tack exactly when their next tack will be but have picked out a reference mark to tack to.

Losers just tack, without having decided by looking around exactly how far they are going to tack, and wind up wasting speed and distance adjusting to the new tack.

Rounding Marks

Winners round the mark somewhat widely and smoothly without a speed reducing slide or the risk of bad crowding.

Winners decide for themselves **before** they get to one mark what will be the best course to the next mark.

Losers follow the pack around the mark without planning, without realizing the guy ahead may be doing it completely wrong.

Sailing Downwind

Winners aren't afraid to tack downwind and travel a longer distance to get a shorter time.

Losers come around the mark toward the downwind leg and while deciding what to do next lose their momentum—which is harder to regain downwind than on any other leg.

General

Winners don't seek instantaneous peak speed so much as high and steady average speed all around the course.

Winners stay clear of others, not only to avoid the emotional side effects but to avoid air turbulence and the chance of collision.

A winner waiting for his next heat to start is frequently watching the race in progress learning from the successes of other winners, the mistakes of losers.

Losers most frequently crowd the race committee to find out what they did in the last race. Winners know they've won.

SAIL-AREA CLASS INFORMATION

There are 10.75 sq. ft per square meter. International racing classes are based on square footage of sail (including profile area of mast and boom) only. However, some one-design classes also have strict body and wheelbase requirements. International racing classes are arranged as follows:

Class I 110-165 sq ft
Class II 70-109 sq ft
Class III 60-69 sq ft In addition, N.A.L.S.A. recognizes:
Class IV 50-59 sq ft
Class V 40-49 sq ft
Class VI 30-39 sq ft

It is recommended that, if you have a variable-area sail, you arrange the reef points so that each area coincides with a specific racing class specification.

How to Build Your Own Landsailer

7

There are always some, in the ranks of people who read a book of this type, who suddenly make up their minds to build a vehicle of their own. The last thing in the world that we want to do is to discourage anyone from constructing a landsailer, but you must keep in mind that just because these things look simple they are not necessarily simple to construct. You must have some training in basic shop techniques, you must have some tools, and you must have some space to do the construction.

The story of the man who had built a boat in his basement and then found that he could not carry it through his narrow door is quite well known. On the other hand, we have even heard of a married couple building an engine-powered airplane in a Brooklyn apartment; so, where there is a will there often is a way.

Before you begin construction, you should expose yourself to as much actual sailing as you can. Visit a number of meets and races, take demonstration rides, and lend a hand to owners of landsailers. Only in this way will you be able to develop a sense of feel and balance that can be translated later to actual design.

When you are irrevocably determined to make your own, jot down the features you'd like. You may say, "I just want to fool around a little bit in the breeze," but if you think this is your only purpose, you are probably fooling yourself. The day will come when you are sailing along, minding your business, and another pilot races past you, only to instill within you an insatiable urge to take off after him. You tighten the sail, corner a little bit faster and...if you're in a contraption, it will fall apart. You must consider performance right from the beginning! Also, some day you may decide to sell your rig and the buyer may have racing in his mind, so make sure that it will be capable of withstanding the stress and strain of hard usage.

With all this in mind, you should now make some sketches. When the sketches begin to look good to you, make some three-view drawings. At least side view and plan view drawings

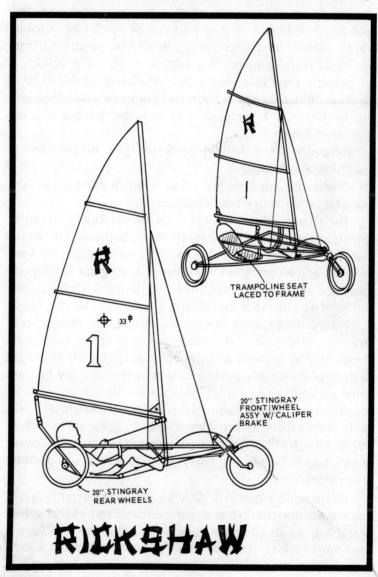

TRAMPOLINE SEAT
LACED TO FRAME

20" STINGRAY
FRONT WHEEL
ASSY W/ CALIPER
BRAKE

20" STINGRAY
REAR WHEELS

RICKSHAW

should be made so that you can check out the location of the center of pressure, center of gravity, any interferences, rigging, seating position, controls, etc. Make the drawings in 1:8 scale (1½ inch to the foot) which is a good scale for this kind of work. You can even make a mockup complete with rigging and sail. Guy wires can be approximated with thread.

Use thin-wall brass tubing, soldered, to simulate welded-tube construction. Most materials can be purchased in hobby stores. (Model landsailer parts can also be purchased from Universal Developments, Box 5253, Orange, Calif. 92667.)

Select a good location for your workshop. It should have plenty of light, a nice even floor, and a table on which the plans can be laid out. If welding is to be done, have a fire extinguisher handy.

Here are some helpful hints for you to consider in designing a landsailer.

Choose the sail area and class in which you plan to race and proportion everything accordingly.

The chassis of the vehicle must be extremely strong to withstand the tremendous forces present. In the chapter on the theory of sail you will be able to find actual figures for wind pressure and forces. Use steel tubes or fiber glass. Aluminum tubes are a lot weaker than steel; for the same strength, you will wind up with more weight with aluminum than with steel.

Follow the practice of airplane fuselage or racecar construction. Triangulate wherever you can to arrive at a strong structure. Use gussets at points of high stress. If you want parts to be dismountable, use bolts of aircraft quality that are twice as large as you first thought they should be. All nuts should have a vibration proofing feature. Nylon inserts are best. Use washers to distribute the loads. Make the structure strong enough to support a very heavy man because you never know who will be using it. This goes double if you are building a two-seater.

On the other hand, to present you with the dilemma facing any vehicle designer, your structure should be light enough so that it will not sink into the sand, or overload the tires. If you need more ballast for strong winds you can always add a jerry can of water on a sandbag for weight.

The axles you use should be made from very strong steel. Surface hardening is desirable. You can use axles from the steering assmebly of small cars or rear axles from trailers. Remember that you may be traveling on two wheels at 50-60 mph on a rough surface—and you certainly do not want to bend or break and axle at such a time.

Wheels and tires usually come from utility vehicles such as minibikes, trailers, etc. These have a conical ball bearing on each end of the hub and can be adjusted, greased, and set up to provide friction-free running without overheating.

Do not use spoked wheels because the tremendous side loads will make the spokes pop out in no time. Solid, die-cast hubs are best. The tires should be inflatable so that you can adjust their pressure for various surface conditions. The harder the tire, the less friction it will create. The softer the tire, the smoother ride you will have.

The tire tread should have circumferential grooves because you want the tire to travel in a straight line and you want it to develop a lot of side force. Knobby tires from minibikes are unsuitable because their original purpose was to create friction and you don't want that. Besides, your tires are not powered, like they are in a powered vehicle. All you want in a good tire is frictionless rolling and high side force.

The bearings in the wheels should be the best quality you can afford. You are going to sail with the wind coming from the side in most instances. There is no centrifugal force (like in a bicycle) to redirect the forces through the hub. The wheel is constantly being pushed sideways and a poor quality bearing will give out in no time.

The mast may be made from varnished hardwood, fiber glass, or steel. If the mast is supported mostly in the bottom it needs to be a lot stronger than a mast which is "stayed" by wires. A certain amount of flexibility is desirable, especially when you flip your vehicle over. Aluminum tubes have been used successfully in small landsailers, but the lower end of the tube must be reinforced by an additional tube inside or outside of the mast tube.

The sail, of course, is one of the most important items in your landsailer. Even if you make everything else yourself, spend a few more dollars and have the sail made by a professional. Make sure he understands the use to which the sail will be put so that he can make the cuts and seams accordingly. While the sail on a sailboat has to be quite baggy, landsailers require relatively flat sails. The forces acting on a land yacht's sail are much higher than those on a sailboat. As a result, stronger seams must be used. The sail material should be about 6-ounce **Dacron**.

Battens in the sail make it possible to employ a curved outline (roach) and thereby increase the sail area. The battens themselves should be very strong because they take up a tremendous load; should they break, they puncture the canvas. For this reason, use the best fiber-glass battens you can buy.

One of the most important features of your landsailer is the steering mechanism. Most of today's landsailers are laid out on a triangular chassis outline with the apex of the triangle in the front and the the base at the rear. The single front wheel is steerable. There used to be landsailers with two in the front and one in the back but this makes for unnecessary complexity in steering.

Four wheels require some sort of suspension (else the chassis will twist) in order to maintain contact with four tires on the ground on rough surfaces. So, the most popular configuration is the triangular chassis with front-wheel steering. This, by the way, makes it easy to triangulate the mast support as well.

As your landsailer is rolling, the front wheel has a tendency to buckle sideways and, for this reason some **caster** has to be built in. "Caster" means that the front wheel will always follow the axis of steering instead of wanting to get out of line. Caster can be achieved in one of two ways: either by locating the front axle behind the imaginary line of swiveling, or by tilting the steering axis.

The first solution is popular when the steering axis is vertical. The second solution is more balanced, stress-wise. This method of castering is employed in bicycles where the front fork is tilted so that its top is farther back than the bottom. When you extend the centerline of this tilted fork you will find that this imaginary line contacts the ground ahead of the contact patch made by the tire. During forward movement, the tire will have a tendency to lag behind the imaginary line of swiveling in much the same manner as a flag flutters behind a flagpole in the breeze.

Think of the front tire as a weather vane and the steering axis as the axle of the weathercock. No matter from which direction the wind is blowing, the weathercock always lines up

with it, because it is balanced to "lag" behind the axle. With a setup of this sort, your landsailer will always track nicely and run true even at high speeds.

An angle of about 5 degrees or so seems to be sufficient. More angle than this makes the chassis drop a small amount whenever the front wheel is swiveled from the dead ahead position. If you want to steer the wheel forward again you have to apply sufficient steering torque to actually lift the chassis. So, use some method of castering but not an excessive amount.

Any other fittings of your landsailer can be made by hand or made up from odds and ends. For instance, a pulley can be made from a clothesline pulley block. Again, use your own judgment; if you have to compromise, place performance first, looks second.

You will spend most of your sailing time sitting in your landsailer. Is it any wonder that experienced pilots equip their vehicles with plush seats? You should use a form-fitting bucket seat so that when you are tilted up or cornering at high speed, your weight will be well supported in a sideways direction.

You should be in a reclining position for several reasons. For one thing you want to cut down on air resistance. For another, you want to maintain a low center of gravity. For another, your entire torso should be well supported so that no part of your anatomy will have a high pressure point (causing a circulation deficiency). Padded bucket seats are best.

In general, keep two things in mind when designing your own landsailer.

1. Complexity usually costs money. It results in a craft that is hard to repair and one that is likely to break down more often. A simple rig usually has less stress on it, is easier to make and repair. Anybody can design a complex monstrosity; elegant simplicity is difficult.

2. Nothing is more disheartening than a breakdown in the middle of a nice sailing day. Nothing beats a ruggedly constructed unit.

Addresses of some places where you can get experienced help and quality merchandise for your landsailer:

Sails:

Windward Custom Sails, 2000 Newport Blvd., Costa Mesa, Calif. 92626

Mel Holman, 5534 Pageland Dr., Toledo, Ohio 43611

Plans for Landsailers:

Honker Landsailers (**Rickshaw** plans)—817 Seventeenth St., Suite 15, Costa Mesa, Calif. 92627

NuSport Mfg. Co. (**Desert Dart** and **Sandsailer** plans)—5221 Rockland, Eagle Rock, Calif.

Lighthouse Landsailer Corp. (**Chubasco** plans)—Box 4672, 17865 Skypark Circle, Irvine Calif. 92707

NALSA (**DN CLASS**)—Box 2283, Newport Beach, Calif. 92660

Windbuggy Mfg.—419 Westminster Åve., Newport Beach, Calif. 92660

Component parts for landsailers.

North American Imports, Mofave, Calif. (rims and hubs for wheels).

DICO Co., 323 East Ball Rd., Anaheim, Calif. 92805 (wheels, axles, bearings, brakes, etc.)

Wilform Buggy Works, 1322 Coronado Ave., Long Beach, Calif. (sealed bearings, hubs, spokes, etc.)   *213-597- 0511*

William B. Sarns (**DN Class** yachts) 3801 Huron Pt., Mt. Clemens, Mich. 48043

Windbuggy Mfg. Co., 419 Westminster Ave., Newport Beach, Calif. 92660 **Windbuggy Class II and III**, also **Fenix Class II.**

Equipment and Maintenance (Some Helpful Hints and Tips)

Have you ever gone on a picnic and found that you have forgotten the bottle opener? Did you ever wish at a baseball game that you had brought along your binoculars? Your enjoyment of a hobby or sport can be greatly enhanced by having proper equipment....when you need it.

And so it is in landsailing. While you could wear nothing but a bathing suit while sailing a starkly equipped landsailer, think of how much more you could enjoy this sport if you had a few pieces of equipment or accessories that the "pros" have. Let me describe briefly some of the items that you will find helpful.

Because you are handling metal equipment and mainly because you hold a rope in your hand whenever you are landsailing, it is highly recommended that you wear **gloves** to prevent rope burns. The gloves you wear should be of the soft leather type with a wrist strap. While it may be fashionable to wear gloves made especially for automobile racing, these are usually too light to be of continued use.

Perhaps the most important item is a crash helmet. Most landsailers have a very low boom which seems to bang into your skull every time you "come about." Unless you are careful, without a helmet you will have a head full of bumps by the end of the day. Your safety helmet need not be very elaborate; however, if you are going to trust your life and health to it, you'd do well to buy the best you can afford.

Goggles are fairly inexpensive and they can prevent tiny sand particles from lodging under your eyelids. Almost any kind of goggles will do as long as they don't scratch easily. Eyeglasses won't do, because they may break or fall off. Secure your goggles to your face by means of an elastic strap.

Fig. 8-1. For your personal comfort use a helmet and gloves.

Before you begin sailing it is advisable to check tire pressures. The gage must be accurate to be of practical use. You should also carry a **tire pump**. In fact, every club should have a pump for its member's use.

Many an experienced landsailor has equipped his vehicle with a **speedometer**. These are similar to the speedometers used on bicycles. You must keep in mind that any device driven by the wheels is going to generate some drag and, as such, it will detract from your top speed.

Sails should never be dumped in a car trunk when not in use. Even if you get an old pillow case it is better than risking a tear or soiling your expensive Dacron cloth. Most sailing supply stores carry **Dacron bags**, or they can be made up to your specifications with the color striping etc. to match your sails.

A **toolbox** is a must to keep your tools together in one place so that when you need them they will be there in good shape. Carry a tire repair kit, a set of wrenches, pliers, some bailing wire, electrician's tape, and bearing grease. A few spare nuts and bolts carried in the toolbox may mean the difference between coming home frustrated or a perfect sailing adventure.

Among the more luxurious items you may like to carry might be a **windspeed indicator**. This may be a simple liquid manometer type or a cup-and-vane rotating indicator which drives a small tachometer generator. A wind velocity meter as well as a wind direction sensor are items that every race committee should have available.

We have recently seen a few landsailors dressed in leather suits much like the ones that motorcycle racers wear. This is good protection against abrasion, wind, and cold. In cold weather you should of course dress warmly and use outer garments which are wind-resistant. In rainy weather or when sailing near the ocean, there is no substitute for all-weather rainwear. This can be obtained in sporting goods stores that sell this kind of outfit to fishermen. Make sure that plenty of ventilation is provided; otherwise, you may perspire and catch cold when evaporation begins.

One of the most important accessories that you will have to purchase or make is a **rack** to be used for carrying your

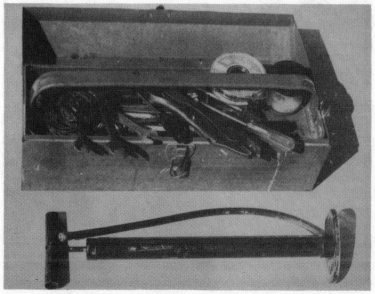

Fig. 8-2. A simple tool kit and tire pump are nice to have along on any sailing outing.

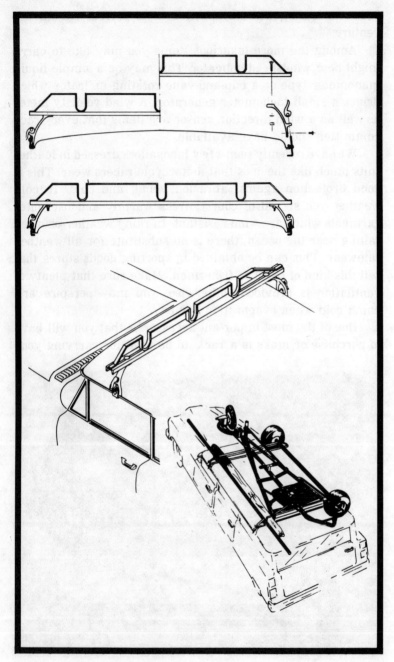

Fig. 8-3. A cartop carrier is a must if you plan to transport your landsailer for long distances.

Fig. 8-4. One landsailer is easy to transport aboard a **Ranchero.**

Fig. 8-5. Two **Chubascos** can be transported on this welded framework made from electrical conduit.

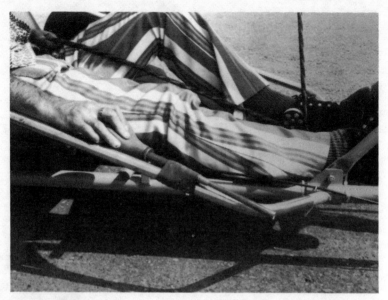

Fig. 8-6. Landsailers are silent...use a horn to warn pedestrians.

yacht atop your car. This may be a simple bar of wood equipped with suction cups. You can make a more elaborate affair to cradle the mast, the chassis, and the rear axle. Whatever type you use, make sure that it is securely fastened to your car. A landsailer chassis is heavy and, if not fastened well, may become a veritable torpedo at any sudden or "panic" stop.

Model Landsailers  9

If you cannot afford to own a full-size landsailer, if you cannot find the time to run it, or if you have no satisfactory location for landsailing, there is a very good compromise available—a radio-controlled model!

While some people associate the word model with shelf replicas of boats or planes, there is nevertheless a class of models that obey the same laws of physics governing full-size vehicles. Such models are fully capable of giving you hour after hour of delightful action.

It is quite possible to build faithful replicas of landsailers even if you only have limited ability. A simple set of tools (screwdriver, pliers, hacksaw) and a few woodworking tools are sufficient to get you going.

Your model will make an ideal science project and it will also be an ideal trainer by which you can demonstrate the various sail positions, sailing methods, and racing techniques. In addition, it will provide you with a hobby which is more relaxing than stamp collecting, more exciting than model cars, less trouble than boats (you never have to wade into the water to retrieve them), as dynamic as model airplanes and yet, without the constant headache of repair.

Running "free," by preset controls, the model will be capable of running in a circle or straight line. When equipped by simple radio control, your model will obey your every wish as it turns and luffs, runs along, tacks, and jibes just like the real ones do, while you control it from 100 yards away. You will be able to sail several models simultaneously around a race course the size of a tennis court.

A SIMPLE MODEL LANDSAILER

If you have a few simple hand tools and are able to scrounge up some scrap materials, you should be able to complete a model an evening.

You will need:

A triangular piece of plywood (12 in. long, 11 in. wide, ½ in. thick)

A square piece of plywood (2 x 2 in., ¾ in. thick)

2 wooden ¼ in. dowels (24 in. long and 12 in. long)

Stiff sheet metal (8 in. long and 1 in. wide, about 1/16 in. thick)

Three wheels with rubber tires (3 in. diameter)

Some sailcloth, glue, screws, nails, axles, etc.

For tools you will need a ¼ in. drill bit, pliers, a saw, sandpaper, hammer, and screwdriver. Add some paint if you really want to go fancy.

Study the overall view of the drawing of Fig. 9-1 so that you get an idea of how the various components are located relative to each other; then, after some careful thought, begin construction. Check Figs. 9-2 and 9-3 to get a good idea of the basic shape and methods of construction.

Glue and nail the small square piece of plywood on top of the triangular piece about an inch from the tip. Allow this piece to dry thoroughly. When it is completely dry, drill a small hole in the square piece from the top and slant the drill a little bit as shown in Fig. 9-4. This hole will support the mast; for best performance it should have a little bit of rake to it, which means that the tip of it is further back than its bottom.

Next, take the long sheet-metal strip and, by holding it near its center with two pairs of pliers, twist propeller fashion. Drill a hole in each tip as well as near the middle of the strip. Now, using woodscrews, fasten the strip under the tip of the large triangular piece of plywood, but make sure that at least 2 in. are left to overhang the tip of the plywood.

For wheels and tires you can use some old tires from discarded toy trucks. Better still, get some model airplane wheels from a nearby hobby store. The manager of the store will gladly explain what kind of axles to use. If you use old toy wheels you can use long nails for axles. Just remember that the wheels must run true, without wobbling; otherwise, the performance of your model will suffer.

The rear wheels can be mounted on long nails stuck into the sides of the triangular piece of plywood. The front wheel is mounted on the protruding end on the metal strip.

Try the chassis by rolling it on the floor. Bend the long metal strip appropriately to make sure that the front tire is vertical and the vehicle runs in a straight line. Put a drop of oil on each axle.

The long ¼ in. dowel should be inserted in the slanted hole on top of the square block. Use a drop of glue if you wish to make this a permanent joint, though a tight fit will do just as well.

Make the sail from a tightly woven light cloth. (If the cloth is too flimsy it will allow air to pass through.) It is best to use Dacron sailcloth for this purpose. You can ask someone to sew a hem into the edge of the cloth so that it will fit around the

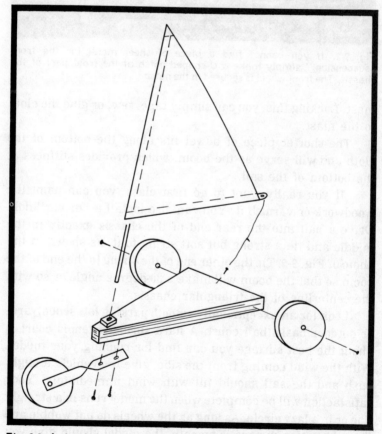

Fig. 9-1. A simple land yacht model can be made from scrap wood, three wheels and a sail. It really works.

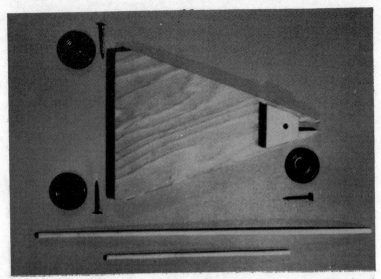

Fig. 9-2. If you cannot find a piece of sheet metal for the front "suspension," simply make a U-shaped notch at the front part of the chassis. The front wheel is secured in the notch.

mast. Lacking this, you can simply tape, sew, or glue the cloth to the mast.

The shorter piece of dowel fits along the bottom of the cloth and will serve as the boom, which provides stiffness at the bottom of the sail.

If you really want to go first class, you can paint the woodwork or varnish it. You can also install a "driver" doll. Drive a nail into the rear end of the chassis exactly in the middle and tie a strong but soft string to it, as shown in the photo of Fig. 9-5. Tie the other end of the string to the end of the boom so that the boom will make a 30-degree angle or so with the centerline of the triangular chassis.

Look for an **exceptionally smooth** parking lot, schoolyard, or outdoor basketball court. A hard surfaced tennis court is about the best surface you can find for running your model. With the wind coming from the side, give the vehicle a slight push and the sail should fill with wind immediately. Your satisfaction will be complete when the model runs in a straight line or in a lazy circle. As long as the wheels do not wobble and the rubber tire surface is smooth, the model should give you many hours of fun.

Fig. 9-3. The elementary landsailer model up-ended here to show construction.

Fig. 9-4. In this case two blocks of wood are glued to the bottom of the chassis to support the front axle.

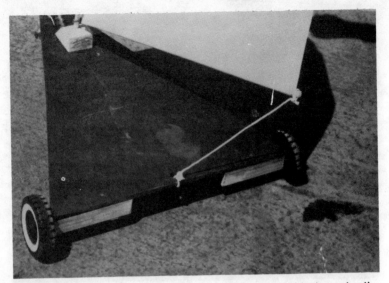

Fig. 9-5. If the chassis is made from thin wood, use two blocks under the rear end of the chassis to support the rear wheels.

Problems such as erratic running should suggest their own remedy. Just make sure that the sail is free to flop from one side to the other when the wind shifts or when the model "comes about," which means that it now shows its other side to the wind.

THE COMMERCIAL MODEL

When you visit the site of full-scale landsailing activities you usually notice an abundance of hand-made models. On inspection you'll probably find that some of them are commercially made; they look professional and they usually perform well. In Fig. 9-6, the two nearer models are "homebrew"; the other two were built from commercial kits.

Once you have tried your hand at making a model landsailer, you will realize that the better your components, the sturdier your vehicle; and the better it is aligned, the faster it will run.

The **Silent Speed** model landsailer, manufactured by Universal Developments, is made for top performance yet it is extremely simple to assemble. (See photo of ad. Fig. 9-7.)

124

As shown in Fig. 9-8, the backbone of the assembly is a sturdy steel chassis, predrilled so that there is no drilling required. The front wheel (Fig. 9-9) is fastened to a steel axle supported by a swiveling bracket (for steering) and a steel wire torsion bar front suspension arm. Assembling these is easy with only a pair of pliers and a screwdriver. The rear axle is a tough piece of music wire sunk into holes at either side of the chassis and held in place by setscrew collars (Fig. 9-10).

The mast support tube is located at the front of the chassis and held between two tongues with a small screw and nut. The top of the tube is straddled by two stamped-steel members. These members actually form a triangular structure as they connect to the side of the chassis. When you hold the tube in one hand and try to twist the chassis with the other you will find it virtually impossible to warp the structure. It seems that just about any kind of wind load can be accommodated without a change in chassis alignment.

The wheels have a patented center locking feature which means that to mount them on the axles one simply presses

Fig. 9-6. Model yachting competition is fun when several modela show up at the "race."

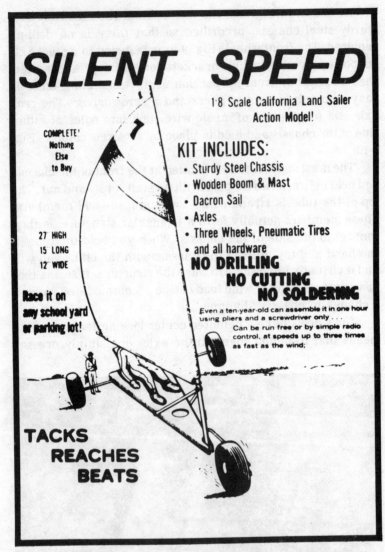

SILENT SPEED

1:8 Scale California Land Sailer
Action Model!

COMPLETE!
Nothing
Else
to Buy

KIT INCLUDES:

- Sturdy Steel Chassis
- Wooden Boom & Mast
- Dacron Sail
- Axles
- Three Wheels, Pneumatic Tires
- and all hardware

NO DRILLING
NO CUTTING
NO SOLDERING

Even a ten-year-old can assemble it in one hour
using pliers and a screwdriver only . . .

Can be run free or by simple radio
control, at speeds up to three times
as fast as the wind;

27" HIGH
15" LONG
12" WIDE

Race it on
any school yard
or parking lot!

TACKS
REACHES
BEATS

Fig. 9-7. **Silent Speed** is a commercially made model landsailer.

them smartly onto the axles and they hold themselves in
place. To remove them you pull the wheels off forcefully. In
normal operation, the wheels spin freely without wobble.

The main mast comes in two pieces (so that the sailer can
be packed in a small box for shipping); the two halves are
connected by inserting them into a brass ferrule tube. With a

drop of glue (or simple pinching of the tube) you can retain the two halves together.

The sail is made from machine-sewn 4 oz **Dacron** sailcloth. You simply insert the mast into the seam along the edge of the sail, which slides down to hold itself in place. The boom is similarly slipped into the seam at the bottom of the sail. A wire hook locates the boom at the right position relative to the main mast.

All that remains now is to bend up the tab at the rear of the chassis (to form a seat back to accommodate a "driver"), and tie a string between the end of the boom and the seatback.

The instructions that come with the kit are very complete and illustrated so that anyone can assemble it in less than an hour. There is nothing else to purchase, drill, solder, or sew. For more information, you should send 25 cents for an illustrated catalog of unusual hobby items to: Universal Developments, Box 5253, Orange, Calif., 92667. The company also has a streamlined body to cover the chassis as well as a driver figure, the two of which really make this kit look realistic as shown in Fig. 9-11.

If you live near an ice-covered pond, you should be able to convert your **Silent Speed** model into an iceboat by the addition of steel runner which mounts on or replace the tires.

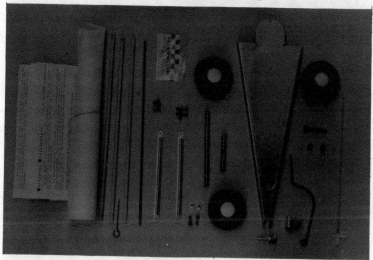

Fig. 9-8. All parts of the **Silent Speed** are precision made. There is nothing else to buy or make. No cutting or soldering required.

Fig. 9-9. When the front wheel is properly set, your elementary land yacht will sail in a circle or straight line.

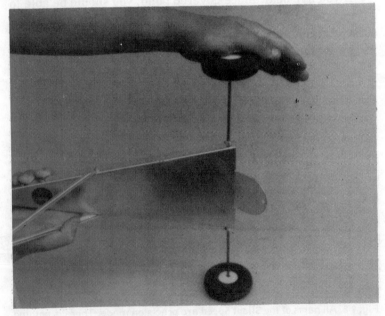

Fig. 9-10. The wheels are simply pressed on to the rear axle.

RADIO CONTROL FOR MODELS

Radio control, contrary to its scary name, is much easier to understand than most people think. You have seen model airplanes being controlled with great accuracy by their "pilots," who stand on the ground up to a mile away from the plane. Similarly, your model landsailer can be controlled from a distance.

The model radio control system consists of the following components: A hand-held transmitter, a receiver (in the model) and a battery, plus one or two "servos," which move the control rods that steer the model or control its sail. The photo of Fig. 9-12 shows a typical receiver mounted below the chassis of a commercial model; Fig. 9-13 shows a pair of "sailors" holding the transmitter control boxes.

The transmitter is a plastic or metal box about the size of a small cigar box. It has one or more control levers on it (or a steering wheel) which are held by the operator. There is an antenna protuding from the top of the transmitter which sends out signals. A dry battery inside the transmitter powers its electronic components. There is a switch also which can be turned on whenever you are ready to send out signals. It should be turned off when not in use to conserve the battery.

There is nothing mysterious about radio control. As the photo of Fig. 9-14 shows, even the youngest of hobbyists can pilot a landsailer.

When the control transmitter is turned on, it sends out a series of inaudible beep-beep signals much like a Morse code. As you turn the steering wheel or move a control lever, the signal becomes slightly distorted so that either the "beeps" or the pauses between them become shorter or longer. If you could hear this signal on a properly tuned in radio receiver, it would sound like a superfast telegrapher sending out a long message.

There is an antenna in the model landsailer. The antenna may be as simple as an insulated wire placed inside the seam of the sail along the vertical mast. The signal sent out by the transmitter is intercepted by this antenna and sent down to the tiny receiver.

Fig. 9-11. A streamlined body is also available from Universal Development.

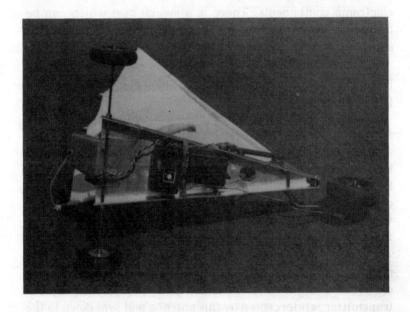

Fig. 9-12. Radio control can be installed very easily under the chassis.

130

By means of colored wires leading from the receiver, one or more servos are connected to the receiver. Each servo has a small electric motor which, by means of an elaborate gear train, drives a wheel or arm outside the servo.

As the signal sent by the transmitter changes as a result of you moving the control levers, the receiver "commands" the servo arms to move exactly and proportionally to your control movements.

The various components of the radio merely plug into each other. Even if you have trouble replacing a fuse in your house, you will have no problem hooking up the radio. Absolutely no previous electronic knowledge is required.

Fig. 9-13. Two young "pilots" prepare to run their models by radio.

Fig. 9-14. Even a child can learn easily how to remote control his model.

Your radio set usually comes in a large box with full instructions. When you turn the switches on (in the transmitter and receiver) and plug the servos into their respective sockets, you should be able to see the servo arms move every time you move a control lever on the transmitter. Immediately the whole thing becomes quite clear to you! All you have to do is imagine a control rod connected between a servo and a component in the model sailer (e.g. steering or sail and you can visualize that, as you stand in one place and steer the transmitter, the model will steer exactly in the same manner.

Radio sets can be purchased by mail order or from hobby stores. A good set with two controls will cost you about $125. There is usually a battery charger included so that you can use the set over and over again. Multifunction sets can provide up to six servos to control every conceivable part of your model (including the "driver's" body for the ultimate in realism); these may cost up to $300. The set offered by Universal Developments, with two servos, sells for $79 complete. All you have to purchase is batteries.

Just about all **digital proportional** radio sets (where the servo moves exactly as you move your controls) are superheterodyne receivers which means that several sets can be operated simultaneously. Thus, up to 10 models can be raced at the same time under separate control of their drivers.

If the transmitting power of your radio is below 100 milliwatts, you won't need a radio license. However, if you own a set which has more power, you will. The Federal Communications Commission requires that owners of such model radio transmitters get a license by applying to one of the field offices. The license fee is $20; no examination is required, and you are all set for five years. You must be a U.S. citizen over 18 to apply for a license.

The six most popular transmitting frequencies are in the popular "citizen band." In order to distinguish one frequency from the other, courteous modelers attach a flag to their antenna, the color of which indicates the frequency of operation. If you see a flag similar to your own, you must not turn your set on because it will interfere with the other man's signal, and vice versa. If you own an amateur radio license (examination required), there are seven more frequencies available. The table of Fig. 9-15 lists the frequencies (amateur and CB) and their flag color codes.

How To Install Your Radio Control

The installation of a radio control set is quite simple. Mount the servos above or below the chassis in the sailer by means of metal brackets and screws or, simply sticking them to the chassis with double-backed servo tape (plastic tape commonly used for mounting mirrors, etc.).

After the servo and the mounting surface have been cleaned of all oil and dirt, simply press the tape on the servo, remove the green paper, then press the servo in place at the appropriate location. A simple wire pushrod serves as connecting rod between the servo arm and the steering mechanism.

To actuate the sails, you may want to mount a large arm on the servo and tie the string to it. By moving the servo arm

FREQUENCY, MHz	COLOR
26.995	Brown
27.045	Red
27.095	Orange
27.145	Yellow
27.195	Green
27.255	Blue

AMATEUR BAND

51.20	Black-Blue
53.04	Black-Violet
53.10	Black-Brown
53.20	Black-Red
53.30	Black-Orange
53.40	Black-Yellow
53.50	Black-Green

OTHER FREQUENCIES

72.16	These three frequencies have
72.96	been allowed recently for model
72.32	vehicle use and color code up to the individual club's discretion.

Fig. 9-15. Color codes for radio-model flags.

the boom will move in and out tightening or loosening the sail as required.

The receiver should be packed loosely in foam rubber and then fastened to the chassis with rubber bands. This is so that any road vibrations will not be transmitted to the delicate parts of the receiver. The battery can also be rubber banded to the chassis. It is best to mount the radio components under a racing body if your model has one or, in the case of the **Silent Speed**, under the chassis where there is plenty of room. The instructions are quite complete in this regard. Figure 9-16 shows the complete "RC" setup—the hand-held transmitter, the driver-carrying landsailer, and the operator. In Fig. 9-17, the relative sizes of the component parts are pictured.

In general, the operation of the radio control set is quite simple once you have connected all components and operated the set in front of you before it is mounted in your model.

Maintenance of the radio set is simple. You will be able to run the radio for an hour or two on every recharge. After each run, turn the set off to save the battery. As soon as you get home after a good run hook up the batteries to a charger.

Fig. 9-16. With a doll installed, the **Silent Speed** looks very realistic.

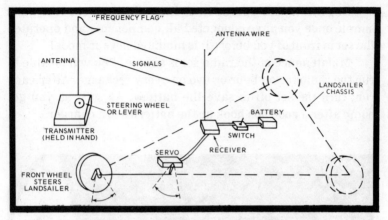

Fig. 9-17. Schematic diagram of model radio control.

Keep dirt and water off the components and make sure that connector plugs are clean. No part of the antenna wire metal should touch metallic chassis parts. Use plastic covered wire for this purpose.

It is entirely sufficient to use radio control only for the purpose of steering the car. As long as the boom is free to swing around, it will "come about" by itself every time you change directions. Sometimes, as when the model "two-wheels" itself (Fig. 9-18), control might get a bit sticky, however.

Once you have adjusted the basic length of the boom string you can usually leave it that way. Steering movements of the front wheel should be very gentle, about 15 degrees from straight ahead is entirely sufficient.

Driving a landsailer by remote control is quite simple as long as you remember that when you move the steering wheel on the transmitter to the right the servo will make an appropriate move and the front wheel will turn to the right. Now, suppose you are on the far end of the track and you turn the sailer around. As it is moving towards you, you must keep in mind that, in effect, the radio control allows you to "sit inside the sailer," which means that as you move the steering wheel to the right it still moves the wheel to the right and the sailer turn to ITS right. This may be confusing at first because, when coming towards you, the model's right is actually to your left.

Fig. 9-18. Even models can lift a wheel when the wind is right.

Fig. 9-19. Radio controlled model land yacht competitions are held at the Balboa Peninsula Pier near Newport Beach, Calif.

Fig. 9-20. You don't need radio control to have fun with models.

A little bit of practice and, keeping in mind that you are "sitting inside the model," will help you get accustomed to this fantastic experience.

Other model landsailers

There are two more commercially available model landsailers. One in kit form and one in plan form.

The **Chauncey Mini-Chubasco**, designed by Duffy Chauncey, an 8-year-old, can be sailed free (without remote control) very nicely. It is available for $5 from Chauncey Enterprises, c/o ALSO, Box 4672, Irvine, Calif. 92664.

The plans for a model landsailer patterned after European models (two wheels in front, one in the back) are available from Model Maker Plans Service, 38 Clarendon Road, Watford, Herts, England. Called **Sand-Fairy Ann** and designed by W.P. Holland, this is an elaborate model whose components have to be scratch built from balsa wood. The finished model has a driver figure which (by means of

138

elaborate levers) leans out to the side in a very realistic fashion. There is a weather vane, mounted in the rear of the chassis, which senses the wind and adjusts the steering action accordingly so that the model always runs on a straight course. The mast is pivoted and stayed by three wires.

Needless to say that all model sailers can be equipped with skates and sailed in the winter time. Regattas, with several models participating are usually held on an informal basis as shown in Fig. 9-19. The day may not be too far off when we will see **one-design** and **all-corners** competitions with rigidly controlled rules.

As it stands today, most models be they radio-controlled or the simple triangle of Fig. 9-20, 1:8. The **Silent Speed** is a reasonably faithful 1:8 scale replica of the famous **Chubasco.**

Courses

The race course usually consists of two pylons set crosswise to the prevailing wind, about 150 ft apart. By means of radio control the models sail around the pylons in 10-lap heats.

With free running models one can set the steering to allow the vehicle to run in circles. The time required to complete the circle may be measured. Another race aims at accuracy where the models are set to run straight and are aimed at a target about 150 ft from the start. The model coming closest to the target wins a prize.

Model landsailing is one of the most relaxing and challenging hobbies around. There is a lack of engine noise and smell, expenses are kept at a minimum, and performance is strictly up to the builder's ability. The love of sport and camaraderie are held in higher esteem than sheer speed. In this respect there is not much difference between pilots of models and full-size landsailer vehicles.

Iceboating

It happened on a windy day near an Eastern town, where a long, frozen river paralleled a straight stretch of railroad track. A passenger train stood puffing on the iron rails, while on the frozen river surface a group of people scurried around, tightening wires and ropes on a device which seemed to be a cross between skates and a sailboat. Suddenly, a hush fell on the crowd and the twon's mayor dropped a flag. The sailpowered device accelerated down the ice, and the locomotive let out a couple of mighty hisses, tooted its whistle, and took off after its lightweight rival.

The date was 1888. The occasion was the culmination of a bet between devotees of iceboating and railroaders: "Which vehicle is faster?" When the event was over, there was no question as to who or what was the winner. The iceboat won by a wide margin. Its speed was an unbelievable 144 miles per hour.

The Dutch seem to have been the first iceboaters in the world. Skating is extremely popular in that country because winters are cold, canals are numerous, and the combination of the two produces miles of glass-smooth surface. A 1768 drawing of a Dutch iceboat shows a sloop-rigged affair with a cross-plank up front and a runner at each end. At the rear, a single skate is attached to the bottom of the rudder. This "bow-steerer" design stayed with sportsmen for almost 200 years. It was basically hard to control and had a strong tendency to spin out unless the helmsman hung onto the tiller.

Though iceboating in America dates back as far as 1790, the turn of this century saw a great upswing in American iceboating activities. New York, New Jersey, Michigan, Minnesota, and Wisconsin all had busy clubs going. One iceboat, the "Clarel," reached a speed of 140 mph on the

Shrewsbury River at Long Branch. The "Wolverine," at Kalamazoo, Michigan, set a record by sailing 20 miles downriver and returning to the starting point in less than 40 minutes.

The problem with the stern-steering iceboats was that, at high speeds—especially when a puff of wind caught the pilot unaware—the wind pressure would lift the stern up, causing an immediate loss of steerage. A high-speed spin of this type not only proved irksome to an otherwise exhilarating sport but a safety hazard as well.

The big design break came in 1931 when Starke Meyer of Milwaukee fabricated a hull with the two runners located in the rear and a single runner providing steering in the front— the familiar configuration of wheeled landsailers of modern times. The wind pressure actually presses the front and the offside runner into the ice. The windward runner may or may not lift up; but even if it does, control is not lost. During the past 40 years, iceboats have been built almost exclusively with bow-steering runners.

ICEBOAT DESIGNS

The most popular iceboat design in the world is the **DN**. From a humble beginning in 1936, this simple but effective iceboat spawned several thousands of copies all over the world (including Russia, Poland, Europe, and the United States). A famous evening newspaper, the Detroit Evening News, sponsored a design contest in the mid-thirties, seeking to create an inexpensive, easily transportable, high-performance iceboat incorporating the monocoque front-steerer design. The winning design was the creation of three sportsmen-craftsmen: Joe Lodge, Norm Garrett, and Archie Aarel. This boat was named after the sponsoring organization and even today the class designation is simply **DN**.

At first the class grew slowly with only a few hundred models built around the Great Lakes area. But when a national yachting magazine published **DN** plans, the boom was on. To attest to the ease with which the DN can be sailed (as well as the great equalizer that a one-design class can be)

SECTIONS THRU MAST

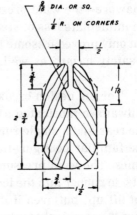

$\frac{9}{16}$ DIA. OR SQ.

$\frac{1}{8}$ R. ON CORNERS

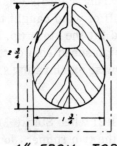

4" FROM TOP

$2\frac{3}{4}$

$1\frac{3}{4}$

$\frac{3}{4}$

$\frac{5}{32}$

$1\frac{1}{8}$

$3\frac{3}{4}$

$\frac{7}{8}$

GLUED JOINT

$1\frac{1}{8}$

$2\frac{1}{4}$

FULL

$\frac{1}{8}$ R.

$2\frac{9}{16}$

3" FROM BOTTOM

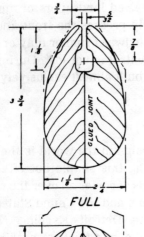

SECTION THRU BOOM

$\frac{3}{4}$

$1\frac{1}{8}$

$2\frac{3}{4}$

$\frac{3}{4}$

$1\frac{1}{2}$

$1\frac{1}{8}$

NO. PCS	SIZE	MAT.	FOR
2	$1\frac{1}{4}$" X $3\frac{3}{4}$" X 16'	SPRUCE	MAST
2	$\frac{11}{16}$" X 7" X 8'	"	PLANK
2	$\frac{5}{8}$" X 8" X 12'	"	FUSELAGE SIDES
1	$\frac{3}{4}$" X 8" X 16'	"	BULKHEADS & BOOM
1	$\frac{1}{4}$" X 18" X 12'	EXT. PLYWOOD	DECK & FLOOR
1	1" X 4" X 10'	OAK	RUNNERS
1	$1\frac{1}{4}$" X $1\frac{1}{4}$" X 42"	"	TILLER
1	1" X 2" X 2'	"	BOOM JAWS
2	$\frac{3}{4}$" X $1\frac{1}{2}$" X 10'	"	SAIL BATTENS
1	$3\frac{3}{4}$" X $4\frac{1}{8}$ X 15	"	STEM & STERN
1	$\frac{5}{16}$" X 35'	ROPE	SHEET LINE
2	LBS WATERPROOF GLUE		ALL JOINTS
1	GROSS 1" NO. 8 FL.HD. SCREWS		FITTINGS
1	" $1\frac{1}{2}$" NO. 10 "	"	& FUSELAGE

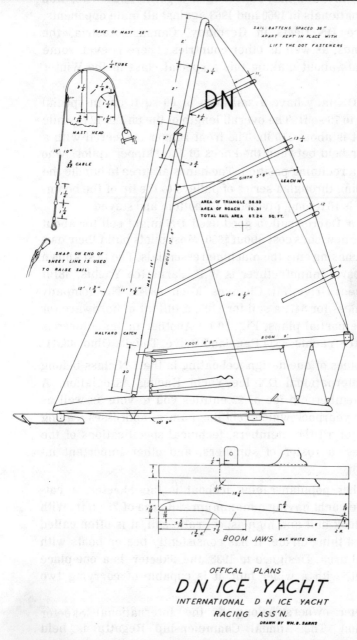

RAKE OF MAST 36"

SAIL BATTENS SPACED 36"
APART KEPT IN PLACE WITH
LIFT THE DOT FASTENERS

¼ TUBE

MAST HEAD

13' 10"
CABLE

SNAP ON END OF
SHEET LINE IS USED
TO RAISE SAIL

DN

GIRTH 5'8"

LEACH 14'

AREA OF TRIANGLE 56.93
AREA OF ROACH 10.31
TOTAL SAIL AREA 67.24 SQ. FT.

HALYARD CATCH

FOOT 8'9"   BOOM 9'

BOOM JAWS NAT. WHITE OAK

OFFICAL PLANS
D N ICE YACHT
INTERNATIONAL D N ICE YACHT
RACING ASS'N.
DRAWN BY WH. B. SARNS

Fig. 10-1. Partial plans of the world's most popular ice yacht, the **DN**.

we should mention that Jane Pegel, a petite housewife, won the Internationals in 1960 and 1963 against all male opponents. There are **DN** fleets in Germany, Canada, Austria, the Netherlands, as well as other countries. There is even some serious talk about making this a special class in the Winter Olympics.

The **DN** may have a sail area of 60 sq·ft ·or, in special cases, up to 79 sq·ft. The overall length of the unit is 12 ft while its weight is about 150 lb. The front runner is steered with a long tiller held between the knees of the skipper (pilot) who assumes a reclining position. The hands are free to handle the rope leading through a series of pulleys to the tip of the boom. The mast is 16 ft long, pivoted at its bottom and stayed.

With a **Dacron** sail, a good used **DN** might sell for about $400 while new ones cost about $650. Most pilots build their own rigs, purchasing only the machined essentials. The best known kit and parts manufacturer is W.B. Sarns Ice Yachts, 38101 Huron Point Drive, Mt. Clemens, Mich. 48043. The company sells runners for $47, a sail for $105, a full kit of hardware for $110. (See partial plans, Fig. 10-1.) Another manufacturer is Holman Ice Yachts, 5534 Pageland Drive, Toledo, Ohio. 43611.

Devotees of one-design iceboating in the **DN** class belong to the International DN Ice Yacht Racing Association. A yearly membership fee of $2 entitles you to vote as well as receive a yearbook which contains names, addresses, racing numbers of all the members, technical specifications of the **DN** class, a roster of suppliers, and other important information.

Another popular racing iceboat is the **Skeeter,** a cat-rigged ice yacht having a maximum sail area of 75 sq ft. With a long, sleek hull and high-aspect-ratio sail, it is often called the fastest thing on ice. It has consistently beaten boats with more sail area. Designed in 1933, the **Skeeter** is a one-place yacht but, with a wider hull, it is capable of carrying two people.

Skeeter owners belong to the International Skeeter Association. The Annual Championship Regatta is held usually on the last weekend of January on a course which measures not less than one mile between marks. The races are for a minimum of six miles, the distance being measured in a straight line between marks. The sail on each racing **Skeeter** must bear the stamp of the official club measurer to certify that it complies with the club rules.

The **Arrow** is an 80 sq ft racer with a fiber-glass fuselage capable of carrying two people. Information on this class can be obtained from M.J. Boston, Mt. Clemens, Michigan.

The **Yankee** is a 75 sq ft yacht designed primarily for home construction. The **Yankee** carries two passengers side by side, and is fully capable of reaching speeds in excess of 100 mph. Information can be obtained from C. S. Peters, 3895 Hylan Blvd., Staten Island, N.Y. The **Chinook** (Fig. 10-2) is the iceboat version of the famous Chubasco landsailer. It carries 55 sq ft of sail. The mainframe is made from welded steel tubes. Fairing for the fuselage can be made by the owner himself. The **Honker iceboat** (Fig. 10-3) is the skate-equipped vehicle made by Honker Landsailers of Costa Mesa, Calif. This boat carries 43 sq ft of sail and weighs 65 lb. For light air, a 60 sq ft sail is also available. The unit is constructed from aluminum tubes and can be transported easily.

The **Viking**, available in completed or kit form from One-Design Marine Inc. 3100 Highway 37 East, Toms River, N.J. 08753, is a two-seater "luxury" iceboat (Fig. 10-4) with a sail area of 66 ½ sq ft and a hull spread of 14 ft by 33 in.

Most of the other iceboats that you would see at a typical race are probably constructed in home workshops by amateur craftsmen. The bow-steering design seems to be most prevalent. The mast may be made from wood, steel, aluminum tube, or fiber glass.

The "plank" deserves special attention as it serves a very important function. The plank is usually a strong piece of wood, usually laminated to provide maximum strength, fastened to the bottom of the hull, as shown in the photo of Fig. 10-5. At the extreme ends are fastened the steel runners which are pivoted so that whenever the iceboat lifts up one of its runners, the runner on the leeward side will be able to assume a suitable angle parallel to the ice surface.

The runners (Fig. 10-6) are made from high-strength steel. The bottom edge of the runner is beveled so that the actual running edge is knife-like. The angle of the bevel is such

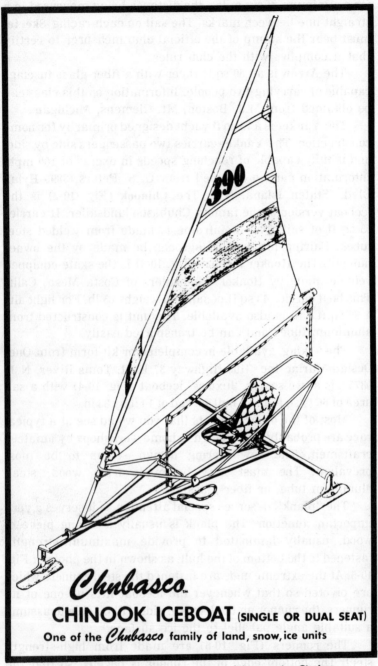

CHINOOK ICEBOAT (SINGLE OR DUAL SEAT)

One of the *Chubasco* family of land, snow, ice units

Fig. 10-2. The **Chinook** is the ice version of the popular **Chubasco**.

that it may make an angle of 40,45, or even 50 degrees to the ice.

The iceboat sails along on runners or skis, depending on surface conditions. Most vehicles are easily adaptable to hard-packed snow or clean ice, because the ice runners are engineered to accept bolted-on skis, as shown in Fig. 10-7. If the bolt-on philosophy is carried through all the way, a very high degree of weather compatibility can be designed into the yacht. The photo of Fig. 10-8, for example, shows an ice runner with a bolted-on ski. By removing the entire runner assembly

Fig. 10-3. An ice-ready **Honker.** Unit weighs less than 75 lb.

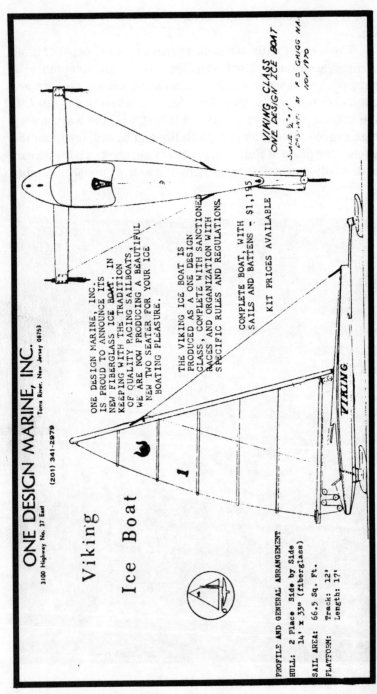

Fig. 10-4. Another popular ice yacht is the **Viking**. Carries two people.

Fig. 10-5. The late Cal Smith at the helm of his **DN** ice yacht. Note that pilot's seat is positioned over plank.

Fig. 10-6. Skates replace wheels on the **Honker.** Ski is attached to skate.

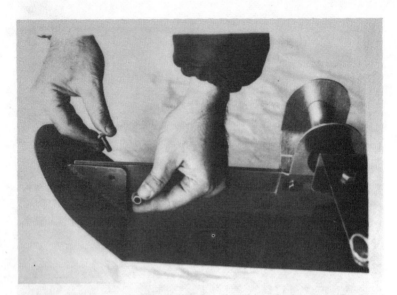

Fig. 10-7. By the use of two 5-16 bolts, the ski is fastened to the front steering skate of the **Honker.**

Fig. 10-8. The wheel of the **Honker** fits onto the axle without modification.

from the vehicle's axle, a land wheel can be slipped on in its place; thus, the unit is convertible from land, to water, to ice boating applications.

Most skippers agree that an iceboat's performance is about 40 percent "sail and rigging" and 60 percent "runners and alignment." The two runners at the tip of the plank must be in absolute parallel alignment to each other and to the centerline of the hull.

One may see all kinds of elaborate gadgets used by the constructors to assure perfect alignment. Any "toe-in" or "toe-out" condition will create unwanted drag. Similarly, a dull edge on the runners will create drag. The wind strength and sail area of an iceboat is about the same as a landsailer; the main difference is in the drag at the running surface. Steel running on ice has a very low coefficient of friction; however, the running edge itself must not have a tendency to scrape the ice during forward movement.

The plank is made in such a manner that it has an upward bow in it when the boat is empty. With the skipper aboard and in a light wind the plank should assume a straight and horizontal position under acceleration, there should be a slight downward sag at the middle. An observer with an experienced eye can easily detect faults in construction or sailing techniques simply by observing the bend in the plank under various sailing conditions.

RACING

Racing is usually conducted on a simple course between two markers set about a mile apart. One of the markers is directly downwind from the other. Thus, the boats have to tack upwind in a zigzag fashion around the upwind mark and then tack back downwind towards the downwind marker. The sailing speeds under these conditions are extremely fast, requiring great skill. As shown in the photo of Fig. 10-9, sailing on ice is "close-hauled"—that is, with the boom closest to the centerline of the hull. This is because the apparent wind is almost from dead ahead due to high speeds attained.

The turn at the weather mark is made fairly quickly while the turn at the lee mark is made gradually to maintain

Fig. 10-9. Sailing on ice is "close-hauled" because the apparent wind comes from dead ahead. Note the planks: one is bowed while the other is straight, indicating proper trim.

maximum speed for the longest time without capsizing or skidding.

One of the greatest thrills of iceboating is the tremendous acceleration (in almost total silence) that the iceboat is capable of. It is much like what you would feel in an elevator if the cable were cut.

Lifting one of the runners is a favorite maneuver; however, it is not conducive to higher speeds. When one of the runners lifts up and a dangerous hiking angle is reached, the skipper slackens the sail for a brief moment, but fully, to regain his balance.

The race is usually started with the boats lined up abreast on the starting line (Fig. 10-10). If there are many competitors, some of the boats may go on a port tack while the other group may start out on a starboard tack. Also, when the competitors are started out in heats (called "flights"), the various groups take off at intervals of seven minutes.

At a given signal, the competitors push their boats and when proper speed is achieved they jump in, strapping themselves in while steering the tiller with their knees. "Braking" is done simply by facing into the wind and allowing the sail to luff. Some simple "scrape" brakes have been used on home-made iceboats. For parking, a loop-like steel attachment on the front runner is made to protrude downwards from the front runner.

As can be seen in the photo of Fig. 10-11, the attire of the skippers reflects a respectful attitude towards the elements. Exposure to the biting wind at high speeds seems to allow the cold to penetrate to the very bones of the competitors. Flight boots, fur lined jump suits, heavy gloves, and the like are the order of the day. Most modern competitors wear outfits ddesignedfor snowmobiling. Thermal underwear, with ffle-design knitted construction, is a must. Most racing clubs require that the competitors wear an approved crash helmet as well.

The future of iceboating is very bright indeed. There are exciting developments in the offing, mainly in the area of reducing wind drag by the use of streamlined fairings. Sails seem to be taller and narrower with full battens to take ad-

Fig. 10-10. A one-design race for **DN** yachts about to start.

vantage of the high aspect ratio, much like the wings of sailplanes. Europeans have been working for the last 25 years— especially in Poland, Estonia, and Germany. These have proved capable of astonishingly high speeds and good control, but they tend to have difficulty in light airs.

Fig. 10-11. Note the winter outfit of ice-sailors. Here a **Chinook** is being assembled prior to a fast run on a frozen lake.

INTERNATIONAL DN ICE YACHT RACING ASSOCIATION

1. BASIC SPECIFICATIONS

The following specifications apply to DN Class ice yachts.

FUSELAGE	PLANS	TOLERANCE Plus	Minus
1. Length overall	144"	3"	3"
2. Beam	19-½"	2"	2"
3. Thickness of decks and cockpit floor	¼"	0"	⅛"
4. Thickness of optional bottom	¼"	0"	⅛"
5. Sides and bulkheads	¾"	¼"	⅛"
6. Aft end of cockpit (intersection of seat back and floor) to pivot pin of steering runner.	110-¼"	0"	12"
7. Distance from bow to front of cockpit	60"	6"	6"
8. Stem block length	10"	Optional	
9. Stem width at bow	2-¾"	1"	¾"
10. Stern block length	4-¼"	Optional	
11. Stern width at stern	1-¼"	2-¾"	0"

12. Seat backs shall be raked aft at an angle of 45 degrees plus or minus 10 degrees. They may be hinged for access to stowage compartment.

13. Seats shall be flat measuring 11" in length at centerline; no maximum height.

14. Depth of side panel at each fuselage station shall not be less than heights in "Layout of Side Panel" on plans.

15. A. Bottom heights of side panels shall not exceed a maximum of 1" above zero line and ⁄ or a maximum of ½" below zero line. Zero line shall be established by a straight line tangent to stem and stern on bottom.

B. Maximum height of side panels above zero line may be 8—½" including deck and bottom covering. All maximum heights of side panels shall be proportional to height as shown in "Layout of Side Panel" on plans.

16. Hull cross sections must be rectangular from a point 6" from the bow to a point 6" from stern.

17. Cockpit floor shall be installed as shown in plans; cockpit bottom **must** be on top of listings. A minimum of 2 knees must be installed.

18. Structural members such as longerons, stringers, knees, listings, bulkheads, bottom, deck, etc. may be added.

19. Design of the internal structure of the fuselage is optional.

20. Grab rails may be installed on the outside vertical surface of the side panels. They may not exceed beyond 8" either end of cockpit. Rails shall not exceed 1" in depth or width. Rails are exempted from fuselage measurements.

21. Steering post and chock may be inclined in the vertical plane of symmetry.

22. Steering shall be accomplished by means of a tiller. Tiller may be of any length or shape. Material is optional.

23. Ballast, if used, shall be permanently installed.

24. Fuselage shall be constructed of wood only. (Sitka spruce, oak and plywood—exterior marine or aircraft—are recommended). Fiberglass may be added for reinforcement only.

Runner Plank

		Plus	Minus
1. Length overall	95"	1"	1"
2. Width at centerline	7"	½"	½"
3. Thickness at centerline	1-⅜"	¼"	¼"
4. Width at ends	5-¾"	1-¾"	¼"
5. Thickness at ends	1-⅜"	¼"	⅜"

6. Cross section is optional

7. Runner plank shall be constructed of wood. Sitka spruce is recommended. Fiber glass may be added.

8. When boat is at rest with skipper **not** aboard, the underside of the runner plank shall be higher at centerline than the underside at outboard ends.

FUSELAGE	PLANS	TOLERANCE	
		Plus	Minus

Mast

1. Length overall (including hardware)	192"	0"	6"
2. Width--measured from full section above boom jaw area to mast hound.	3-¾"	¼"	¼"
3. Thickness--measured from mast step to mast hound	2-¼"	¼"	¼"

4. Only one bolt-rope tunnel is permitted. The bolt-rope tunnel shall be substantially straight with the mast relaxed. Tubing or track prohibited.

5. Cross section profiles are optional. Mast may be hollow.

6. Width and thickness above mast hound is optional.

7. A full length halyard must be installed. An internal halyard is permitted.

8. Devices which prevent or hinder movement of the boom on the mast are prohibited.

9. Mast shall be constructed of wood. Sitka spruce is recommended. Number of laminations is optional. Fiber glass may be added.

Boom

1. Length (from mast)	108"	0"	optional
2. Depth (from outhaul bracket to 12" from mast)	2-¾"	¼"	¼"
3. Thickness (from outhaul bracket to 12" from mast)	1-½"	¼"	¼"

4. Only one bolt-rope tunnel is permitted. The bolt-rope tunnel shall be substantially straight with boom relaxed. Tubing or track prohibited.

5. Cross section profile is optional. Boom may be hollow.

6. Boom jaws are required. Devices which prevent or hinder movement of the boom on the mast are prohibited except for check wire.

7. A ½ inch wide strip shall be painted around the boom in contrasting color. Stripe shall be perpendicular to sail tunnel. Forward edge of the stripe shall be 8', 10" or less from forward inner surface of sail slot, projected fairly to black band.

	PLANS	TOLERANCE Plus	Minus

Runners

1. Steel plate type (steel body with stiffening elements).

		PLANS	Plus	Minus
a.	Plate thickness	.25"	.020"	.020"
b.	Length	29-½"	½"	3-½"
c.	Height	5"	0"	1"
d.	Thickness (contained by chock)	1"	1/32"	1/32"

e. Length, material, location and cross section of stiffening elements are optional

f. Method of attaching stiffening elements is optional.

g. Type of steel plate is optional.

2. Wood type (wood body with attached steel angle, "T" Section or triangular steel section). This means commercially available section. Technical Committee will rule against any special fabrications.

		PLANS	Plus	Minus
a.	Thickness of body	1"	1-32"	⅛"
b.	Length	36"	0"	6"
c.	Height	4-⅛"	⅞"	⅛"
d.	Thickness contained by chock	1"	1-32	1-32"

e. Body shall be made of wood. Oak is recommended. Fiber glass may be added.

3. Profile of runner is optional with the exception that front ends of all runners shall have ⅝" radius or larger.

4. Runner stiffening elements shall not project laterally more than 3" from runner edge.

5. Steering runner shall be equipped with a parking brake.

6. Weight of any individual runner shall not exceed 17 lbs.

7. Method of attaching runner to chock and chock to plank shall be accomplished as shown in plans.

158

9. Runner edge angle, camber (crown) and shape of contact line are optional.

10. Each yacht shall be restricted to the use of 3 sets of runners during a regatta.

11. A maximum of four holes, which are not structurally required, may be drilled in each runner. Hole diameters shall not exceed ½" diameter.

Runner Base and Cut (Track)

	PLANS	TOLERANCE	
		Plus	Minus
1. Longitudinal distance from pivot axis of steering runner to pivot axis of aft runner	100"	3"	3"
2. Lateral distance between aft runner edges	95"	0"	optional

below pivot axis (to be measured with skipper in cockpit in sailing trim)

Sail

1. Material may be of nylon, cotton or dacron. If used, Dacron shall be 6.5 oz cloth manufactured by Howe and Bainbridge with cloth 36" wide or less.

2. Hoist shall be 14 feet or less.

3. Foot shall be 8'10" or less.

4. Leach shall be 14' or less.

5. Girth shall be 5'8" or less excluding bolt rope.

6. The width of the headboard shall be 4" or less. The overall dimension of the head of the sail, including bolt rope shall be 5-½" or less.

7. Spacing between battens shall not exceed 36", nor be less than 32".

8. Batten pockets shall lie at 90 degrees plus or minus 5 degrees to the leach.

9. Batten material, length and structural characteristics are optional.

10. Sail may have one row of reef points.

11. A yacht is restricted to the use of one sail in a regatta.

12. Altering the sail characteristics, such as area and camber, during a regatta by any means other than the natural flexing of structural members and positioning the clew grommet on the outhaul bracket are prohibited. This includes reefing. Batten adjustment is excluded.

13. Yacht number and the letters "DN" shall be affixed to each side of the sail. Color of numbers and "DN" shall contrast with sail and be a minimum of 10" high.

14. A transparent window shall not exceed 300 sq inches.

15. A steel cable, at least 3-64 in. in dia shall be attached to headboard, running inside the luff to a point outside the sail at the tack. Lower end of the cable shall form a loop which must be secured to tack pin on boom when under sail. Distance from top of headboard to center of ¼" bolt inserted in the loop shall not exceed 14' with cable straight and under 10 lb tension.

16. Sail shall not extend aft of the forward edge of the ½" boom stripe which is located 8'10" from the forward edge of the mast slot.

17. The leach, defined as the distance between the centers of ¼" bolts inserted in the head board hole and clew grommet, shall be measured with the sail free of battens and under five pounds tension.

18. The girth (distance between the luff midpoint and the leach midpoint excluding bolt rope) shall be measured with the battens removed and such tension as is required to remove wrinkles. Mid-points are found by folding the sail so holes line up and marking the fold.

Rigging

1. Framing stays are prohibited. Any cable not shown in plans is prohibited.

2. All stays shall be steel cable and shall be ⅛" or greater in diameter.

3. Halyard shall be steel cable and shall be 3-32" or greater in diameter.

4. Full length bobstay shall be installed and anchored on stern block or immediately in front of plank. Bob stay strut must be at least 4" in ht.

5. Tubes and other means of rigid adjustment of stay lengths are permissable.

6. Devices which adjust stay lengths while yacht is under-way are prohibited.

7. Means for rigid adjustment of mast step location are permissable.

8. Means for adjustment of mast step location while yacht is under-way are prohibited.

9. Mast step shall be rigidly mounted on the deck of the fuselage.

10. Mast step shall permit free orientation of mast.

	PLANS	TOLERANCE Plus	Minus
11. Horizontal distance from mast step pivoting point (center of ball) to pivot axis of steering runner.	37"	4"	2"
12. Horizontal distance from pivot axis of steering chock to pivot axis of steering post.	46"	4"	2"
13. Distance from lower mast hound bolt to base of mast	133-½"	6"	6"

14. Six sheet blocks shall be installed.

15. 4 sheet blocks shall be installed aft of the rear limit of cockpit floor; 2 on boom; 2 on fuselage.

16. One sheet block shall be located forward on the boom within 1' of mast.

17. One sheet block shall be installed on the tiller post.

18. The sheet must be attached to the boom and pass through all blocks as shown on plans.

19. Blocks must be individual and have fixed positions of fuselage and boom.

Fittings

1. Diameter of the sheaves of the sheet blocks shall not exceed 4 inches.

2. One of the six required blocks may incorporate a one-way feature.

3. Steering chock may incorporate a shock absorbing feature.

4. Hardware need not conform to plans as long as specifications are not violated and hardware performs the same function that the plan item performs.

5. Side Chock

		Plus	Minus
a. Width of runner slot	1-1-32''	1-32''	1-32''
b. Depth of chock	3''	½''	⅛''
c. Length of chock	7''	2''	¼''

6. Mast Step

		Plus	Minus
a. Height of pivoting point (center of ball) above deck	1-⅜''	¼''	¼''

7. Location of halyard catch on mast is optional.

8. Halyard must be capable of lowering and raising the sail with yacht in upright position.

9. Additional fittings to secure halyard to mast are permissable.

10. Only one mast, boom, fuselage and runner plank may be used for an entire regatta, unless broken beyond reasonable repair (as interpreted by race committee.)

2. DN ICE YACHT CONSTRUCTION PROCEDURE & POINTERS

Fuselage

Lay out the side panel on one piece of stock and the vertical lines for the stations on both pieces. Nail these pieces together with the lines on the outside and cut to contour. Cut the bulkheads, seat back, stem, and stern. To assemble, fasten the sides to the stern block, leaving the lines on the inside. Use 1-½'' No. 10 screws and glue on all joints. Next, fasten the No. 9 bulkhead in place. Cut out and fit the plywood for the cotpit floor. Screw the ¾'' square listings in around the edges, then the floor. Now the listings at stations 5, 6, 7, and the cotpit knees. You may cut the decks, leaving stock on the outside edges to be trimmed off after it is screwed down with 1'' No. 8

screws, placed 4" apart. When you have the runner plank finished, put the cleats on to fit.

Runner Plank

The stock should be slightly oversize. Finish one edge straight. Draw a line across the center of the plank square with the finished edge, also a parallel line on each end equidistant from the center. Place a saw horse under each end. Cut a 2x4 or stick so that when when placed between the center of the plank and the ceiling it will give you a half-inch more crown than desired when finished. You should have 24 wood parallel clamps on hand. Mix 12 oz of waterproof glue and coat each. Place the pieces together and put two clamps on each side of the center, then bend the crown in with the stick from the ceiling. Now, check each end and at center with level. Be sure the level is square with the straight edge. Put the remaining clamps on and recheck with level. After the glue has set, remove the clamps and cut to contour.

Mast & Boom

Finish the tunnel edge straight. Cut the tunnel with a moulding cutter. It is important that the tunnel is sanded well, leaving no rough spots or sharp corners. You will need 24 clamps for the mast and 15 for the boom. Mix 8 oz of glue for the mast and 5 oz for the boom. It is best to glue them with the tunnel up and put the clamps on from the opposite side. Clean the excess glue out of the tunnel by pushing a piece of cloth thru with a stick. After the glue has set, cut to contour and rough the corners off with a circular saw. Then glue in the mast head block. Shape up with a plane and spoke shave and hand sandpaper. Bore the hole in the bottom of the mast and fit the socket in. File a groove in the mast head for the halyard tube to set in. Before drilling the holes for the mast hound, clamp it in place and set the boat up to check the location. You should have 1-½" extra cable on one side stay when the other two stays are tight. Glue and screw boom jaws on with two 2-½" and two 2" No. 12 screws on each side.

Tiller

May be made of one piece of 1-¼" sq oak or 2 pieces ⅝ x 1-¼". Put a ¼" bolt through as shown before spreading to put handle in, using two 1-½" No. 9 screws in each side. Use six screws to put filter block in.

Runners, Plate

Cut front end to contour. To machine the crowned edge, clamp the runner so the ends are bent toward the side being cut. To determine the exact amount of bend use this formula: Bend equals desired crown times tangent of angle (as shown on the plans). Next, cut rear end to contour. Cut aluminum to contour and clamp in position; drill and countersink for rivets. The rivets may be cut from ⅜" dia., all 1-⅛" long. File, polish and stone edges. Then drill the 24-64" hole.

Runners, Angle-Iron

Cut wood to contour. The angle is easily cut on a rip saw by setting the blade on a 45 degree angle and passing thru against the fence with the curved edge tangent to the table, in line with the center of the blade. To insure against splitting the runner in use, put two ⅜ dia. x 3-¾" carriage bolts in from the top edge, 3" fore and aft of the 25-64" axle hole. Countersink hex nuts in to clear angle iron. Drill and countersink the angle iron and screw it on, starting at the front end, bending it around as you go. File screw heads flush and finish with a belt sander, then oilstone.

The Future
of Landsailing

In the pages of this book we have looked at the past of the sport of landsailing as well as its present. It is inevitable that as the sport becomes more popular, the ever-inventive genius of the American sportsman-hobbyist will devise new and improved means of enjoying the sport.

With more spare time available to the average working man, the search goes on for leisure activities that satisfy man's need for recreation, competition, and relaxation. In keeping with this trend, there is a veritable explosion in the manufacture of sail-powered products! Witness the sudden popularity of sailboats even with "landlubbers." The need for privacy can easily be satisfied when one is sailing on a vast lake, ocean or desert drylake.

In our quest for more ecologically acceptable pastimes, we look for active sports which do not produce noise and smell. While motorcycles and dunebuggies have their place, they are basically instruments of transportation. A landsailer, on the other hand, is somewhat unpredictable; the relaxation it provides is in the eternal challenge it offers. Landsailers have speed—lots of it. This is an essential element in any modern "action" hobby. But speed is a result of the operator's skill rather than his pocketbook.

Racing, at high or low speeds, is an essential part of landsailing. The ever-changing wind makes racing an exciting and original experiment every time you line up at the starting line. Competition in other sports require a constant output of money, but with landsailing you have very little expense after your initial investment. Fuel is free, while the cost of racing, club membership, and basic transportation to the sailing site for an entire year will probably cost less than a single weekend of skiing, fishing, or hunting.

Landsailing can be pursued by young and old alike, summer or winter. No specially prepared track is required.

You may consider the undependability of the wind and the relative scarcity of sailing sites as negative elements; but what is more fun than planning your trip, preparing your equipment, traveling to the site, or waiting for the wind while chatting with your friends over a glass of beer?

With the above factors in mind, one does not have to ponder the question too long. There is a definite future in landsailing with YOU in the middle of the picture.

Perhaps in a few years our internal-combustion engines will have polluted the atmosphere so much that cars will be "out" and sail-powered vehicles "in." There may be special sailing sites or "sailing lanes" constructed along beaches. There may be instructional classes available to the public, with rental vehicles as commonly available as canoe or bicycle rentals are today.

We need not look too far into the future...as this is being written, the Department of Recreation in Anaheim, Calif. has purchased 20 small landsailers to be used in a special class for children who sail these yachts on the parking lot in front of Anaheim Stadium. Can you imagine the enthusiasm these youngsters will have when they grow up?

Perhaps the future holds interesting developments for the engineering-oriented enthusiast. The Patent Office has recently reported an upsurge in various types of convertible landsailers, "amphicats," "hermaphrosailers," "multisailers," and the like, all of which claim to be convertible for use on land, ice, or water.

Before investing your money in one of these untried contraptions, consider the fact that a water sailer is designed to work efficiently at wind-to-craft speed ratios of 1.2:1 while landsailers run in the range of 1:3. Iceboats, on the other hand, may run as fast as 1:5. Correspondingly, the sails (as well as the general construction of the vehicle) have to be able to utilize the wind differently in each category (land, water, ice) which may be a physical impossibility.

Structural requirements also vary a great deal, depending on application. Waves are slow in comparison with the rapid pounding that a rutted desert floor may mete out to the wheels.

We have arrived at a point where there are serviceable vehicles available commercially for anyone who wants them. You should not deviate from the tried principles just to be different. On the other hand, do not be afraid to prove your ideas in practice if they seem to offer an advantage—this is the challenge of the unknown.

Appendix A
Glossary

SAIL TERMS

Battens—Stiffeners inserted into body of sail to help maintain strength and aerodynamic shape.

Clew—Corner of sail at distant end of boom.

Clew Outhaul—Line joining sail to distant end of boom.

Draft—Natural shaping or curvature built into sail by sailmaker to give proper airfoil and lift. Somewhat adjustable by tack, downhaul, outhaul and mainsheet tension.

> Light Wind—Minimize draft, use "full" sail, tighten battens into pockets.
>
> Medium Wind—Average draft, average tension on adjustments and battens.
>
> Strong to Heavy Wind—Minimum draft, flatten sail and loosen battens.

Foot—Portion of sail over and near boom.

Head—Corner of sail at top of mast.

Leach—Unsupported "after" section of sail between distant end of mast and boom.

Luff—Portion of sail over and near mast.

Roach—Material built into or removed from leach of sail by sailmaker to increase or reduce area of sail.

> Positive Roach—Outward curve of leach for increased area in light to medium winds—supported primarily by battens.
>
> Negative Roach—Inward curve of leach for reduced area in strong to heavy winds—battens not really required.

Sleeve—Portion of sail into which mast or boom are inserted.

Tack—Corner of sail at junction of mast and boom.

> Tack Downhaul—Line joing sail to boom at tack.

BOOM AND TACKLE TERMS

Bail—Metal straps for attachment of tackle. (Three on Boom)

> Outermost Bail—For attaching mainsheet becket block.
>
> Mid-Boom Bail—Run mainsheet through this bail to keep it from dangling.
>
> Inboard or Vang Bail—For future attachment of boom vang.

Block—Don't ever call them pulleys again.

> Becket Block—A block with means to tie off one end of line.
>
> Single Block—A block with one moving wheel (or sheave)
>
> Shackle—Mechanism for attaching block to boom or frame.
>
> Ring-a-Ding—Small "ring type cotter pin" for holding shackle of block together.

SAILING TERMS

Beating—Sail zig zag course on alternate port and starboard tacks with landsailer pointing as much toward the wind direction (upwind) as wind and speed will permit.

Boom Downhaul—Line between inboard end of boom (boom yoke) and fork assembly to prevent boom from "riding up" mast.

Boom Vang—Auxiliary equipment to reduce tendency of boom to "lift" when sheet is eased.

Yoke—Coupling device between boom and mast to which tack downhaul and boom downhaul are also attached.

Come Up or Head Up— Steering to cause the true wind to be more toward the front of the landsailer. For instance, changing from downwind condition to reaching condition.

Coming About—Same as tacking.

Downwind—Sailing on either tack with true wind coming from (or very nearly from) behind the landsailer. Also known as "Running" condition.

Ease Out—To slack off the mainsheet to allow boom and sail to move away from center line of landsailer. A good basic rule to remember is "If in doubt, ease it out."—Always true when starting, worth trying when moving, usually good for slowing or stopping.

Free Off or Ease Off—Steering to cause the true wind to be more toward stern of landsailer. For instance, changing from beating to reaching sailing condition.

Jibe—The action of boom and sail when changing from port to starboard or starboard to port while sailing downwind.

Jibing—Changing sail and boom from port to starboard tack or starboard to port tack with wind coming from behind landsailer (can be performed only in downwind sailing condition).

Landsailer—What one who does it, does it in.

Landsailor—One who does it.

Luff, Luffing, Luffed—Condition when landsailer is pointed nose toward wind with no pressure on port or starboard side of sail.

Mainsheet—Principal line for controlling angle between sail (boom) and wind.

Port—Left side of landsailer when looking forward.

Port Tack—Sailing condition when wind pressure is on port side of sail.

Reaching—Sailing on either tack with true wind coming roughly perpendicular to direction of travel (apparent wind may be well forward.)

    Close Reach—True wind is more forward but landsailer is not beating

    Beam Reach—True wind is nearly perpendicular.

    Broad Reach—True wind is more aft but not dead behind or downwind.

Rope—You should call it a "line." Principal line on **Chubasco** is the mainsheet.

Sheet—See mainsheet.

Sheet In—Pulling on mainsheet to cause boom and sail to move in toward centerline of landsailer—normal action as speed of landsailer increases.

Starboard—Right side of landsailer when looking forward.

Starboard Right Of Way—A landsailer on starboard tack has right of way over landsailer on port tack.

Starboard Tack—Sailing condition when wind pressure is on starboard side of sail.

Tacking—Steering nose of landsailer through the wind direction to change from port to starboard or from starboard to port. Sail with luff (or flutter) at midpoint of tack.

RACING TERMS

Abandonment—An ABANDONED race is one which the race committee declares void at any time after the starting signal, and which can be resailed at its discretion.

Bearing Away—Altering course away from the wind until a machine begins to jibe.

Cancellation—A CANCELLED race is one which the race committee decides will not be sailed thereafter.

Clear Astern and Clear Ahead: Overlap—A machine is CLEAR ASTERN of another machine when the machine is aft in a normal position. The other machine is CLEAR AHEAD. The machines OVERLAP if neither is clear astern; or if, although one is clear ASTERN, an intervening machine overlaps both of them. The terms CLEAR ASTERN, CLEAR AHEAD AND OVERLAP apply to machines on opposite Tacks only when they are rounding or passing Marks and Obstructions.

Close-Hauled—A machine is CLOSE-HAULED when sailing by the wind as close as she can lie with advantage in working to windward.

Finishing—A machine FINISHES when any part of the machine crosses the finishing line from the direction of the last mark.

Jibing—A machine begins to JIBE at the moment when, with the wind aft, the foot of her mainsail crosses her center line and completes the JIBE when the mainsail has filled on the other tack.

Leeward and Windward—The LEEWARD side of a machine is that on which she is, or, if LUFFING head to the wind, was carrying her sail (mainsail). The opposite side is the windward side. When neither of two machines on the same TACK is CLEAR ASTERN, the one on the leeward side of the other is the leeward machine. The other is the windward machine.

Luffing—Altering course towards the wind until head to the wind.

Mark— A Mark is any object specified in the instructions which a machine must round or pass on a required side.

Obstruction—An OBSTRUCTION is any object, including machines under way, large enough to require a machine to make a substantial alteration of course to pass on one side or the other or any object which can be passed on one side only.

On a Tack—A machine is ON A TACK except when she is TACKING or JIBING. A machine is on the TACK (starboard or port) corresponding to her WINDWARD side.

Postponement— A POSTPONED race is one which is not started at its scheduled time and which can be sailed at any time the race committee may decide.

Proper Course—A PROPER COURSE is any course that a machine might sail after the starting signal, in the absence of the machine or machines affected, to FINISH as quickly as possible. The course sailed before luffing or BEARING AWAY is presumably but not necessarily that yacht's PROPER COURSE.

Racing—A machine is RACING from her preparatory signal until she has either FINISHED and cleared the finishing line and finishing MARKS or retired, or until the race has been cancelled, postponed or abandoned.

Starting—A machine STARTS when, after the starting signal, any part of the machine first crosses the starting line in the direction of the mark.

Tacking—A machine is TACKING from the moment she is beyond head to wind until she has BORNE AWAY, if beating to windward, to a CLOSE-HAULED course: if not beating to windward, to the course on which her mainsail has filled.

Appendix B
Sailing Sites

Southern California:

El Mirage Dry Lake, San Bernardino County
Superior Dry Lake, San Bernardino County
Soggy Dry Lake (Near Lucerne), San Bernardino County
Rabbit (Near Lucerne), San Bernardino County
Coyote Dry Lake, San Bernardino County
Holtville (Near El Centro)
Areas open with permission—check with ALSO before using
Mile Square, Fountain Valley
Rancho California, Temecula
Apple Valley Airport
Mojave Airport

California City Airport

Northern California:

Crescent City
Pismo Beach (Eastern Section), San Luis Obispo County
Humboldt Bay Beach Area (Near Eureka)
Upper and Middle Dry Lakes (Near Alturas)

Oregon:

Newport Beach
Florence
Gearhart

Washington:

Pacific Beach Area
Long Beach Area

Nevada:

Ivanpah
Humbolt
Mesquite
Carson
El Dorado (Las Vegas)
Winnemucca
Mud Lake, Tonopah

Utah

Bonneville Salt Flats
Sevier Dry Lake

Arizona:

Red Lake

Wilcox
Virginia Beach, Virginia
Cocoa Beach, Florida
Sea Island, Georgia
Padre Island, Texas
Corpus Cristi, Texas

Mexico:

Estero Beach (Near Ensenada), Baja
La Salina (Near Ensenada), Baja
San Quintin, Baja
San Felipe (Sea of Cortez), Baja
Punta Bunda

as well as hundreds of parking lots around the country.

For up-to-the minute information on sailing events and sites, contact the following American Land Sailing Organization Information Officers:

Orange and San Diego County Area, California

A.L.S.O. National Headquarters, Irvine, CA 714-546-8045
Don Patton 714-534-0420

Los Angeles County, California

Bob Ashlock 213-780-5550
Dave Moeller 213-248-1926

Riverside County, California

Bill Eisenlohr 714-737-3650
Bob Chaffee 714-676-8411

Lancaster — Palmdale — Mojave Area, California

Bill and Sharon Porter 805-948-3186

San Bernardino County, California

Dan Niestradt 714-245-9924

Northern California

Ken Turner — Alturas / Redding—Reno 916-233-3074

Oregon

Mike Taylor — Eugene / Corvallis / Newport Areas 503-688-6488
Dick Gehr — Portland / Arch Cape Areas 503-222-7060

Washington

J.T. Quigg — Hoquiam / Aberdeen / Ocean City 206-533-1530
Bob Langdon — Seattle Area 206-784-7717

Hawaii

Bill Thompson — Honolulu Area 808-533-2408

Appendix C

North American Landsailing Association (N.A.L.S.A.) International Sailing and Racing Rules

In this sport the rule of the road is **right** (la priorite de droite) and stress is laid on this requirement.

These rules may, however, be adapted to meet special conditions arising from direction of the wind and the state of the ground.

Thus a pool, soft sand, a drain pipe, etc., are considered obstacles which it is usual to pass round by tacking.

1. INTRODUCTION

The rules of ordinary sailing are no different from those of racing with the exception of the start, going about, the finish, etc.

2. General

Every yacht is obliged to carry a number on both sides of the sail, the figures of this number will have the following dimensions: Height 25 cm (10"), Width 17 cm (7"), Thickness 4 Height 25 cm (10"), Width 17 cm (7"), Thickness 4 cm (1⅝" approx.). In International Competitions, these figures will be preceded by a latter showing the country of origin. A—Gt. Britain, B—Belgium D—Germany, DZ—Algeria, F—France, H—Holland, NZ—New Zealand, US—States.

This number will also be displayed on each side of the yacht (or on a laterally visible board) the minimum height of the letter and figures being 18 cm (7½").

All yachts must be fitted with a brake (either wheel or ground contact). Every pilot must be equipped with an audible warning of approach.

SAIL MEASUREMENTS: Each National Federation or club is responsible for measuring the sails of its members.

The sails shall be divided into triangles and trapesiums in such a way as to reduce any curved lines in such figures so that the maximum depth of the curve does not exceed 2 cm (0.8").

The total surface thus obtained shall be certified and inscribed on the sail in square meters to the first decimal point; a 3 percent tolerance is admissible when classifying sails into categories.

3. RACING PRELIMINARIES

(a) **Warning:** The WHITE flag is hoisted 30 minutes before the start.

(b) **Entry Conditions**

(1) Entries are accepted from pilots (and copilots where appropriate) up to 15 minutes before the start and must be acknowledged before the start.

★ Based on rules established by the European International Federation of Sand and Land Yachts in 1962 and revised in 1967 and 1968.

PASSENGERS ARE FORBIDDEN.

(2) The yachts must comply with Rule 2 above (General Regulations).

(3) The pilots and copilots must be affiliated to their National Federation or club.

(4) Every pilot, by the fact of entering a race, acknowledges that he understands the Racing Rules and agrees to abide by their conditions.

(5) The wearing of a crash helmet is **compulsory** both for pilots and copilots.

(6) The minimum age for pilots will be laid down in the particular rules for each competition. Persons under 21 years of age must have their parents or guardians permission in order to take part in International Competition. The organizers may demand a written statement from the Federation or Club confirming this permission.

(c) Each yacht must display pennants, RED on the PORT side and GREEN on the STARBOARD side, placed 1½ meters (approx 4½ ft) from the ground.

(d) A GREEN flag with a YELLOW diagonal is the signal for the immediate assembly of the competitors near the race officials.

(e) The BLUE flag is hoisted 5 minutes before the start.

(f) The flags may be replaced by signals of the same color.

(g) A RED and WHITE flag indicates an obstacle or turning marker.

4. STARTING PROCEDURE

(a) The Signal for the Start may be given by a rocket or starting pistol in addition to a RED flag. However, the dropping of the RED flag preceded by a count down of 5 seconds, is the only official starting signal.

b) Competitor may only cross the starting line(s) after the signal has been given. They are allowed to push their yachts up to the starting line(s) but beyond that, Rule 10 below applies.

(c) The Start is made behind the line(s) according to the JURY's instructions. The yachts must be at least 3 metres (approx 19½ ft) between each line of yachts on the starting grid.

When starting wind astern yachts will be stationed perpendicular to the wind direction.

(d) During the whole of the Start the yacht on the right of each competitor is regarded as being OVERTAKEN and must act as such, while the yacht on the left is regarded as the OVERTAKING yacht and must act as such (see RULE 8 below-OVERTAKING).

5. YACHTS MEETING FROM OPPOSITE DIRECTIONS:

When two yachts meet each other face to face, each must go to its right, so as to leave at least 10 meters (approx 11d) between them. However, the yacht with 'wind astern' has priority because of the difficulties of its maneuvers. Wind is defined as 'wind astern' when it makes an angle of 135 degrees or more with the direction of the yacht sailing before it.

6. YACHTS CROSSING:

When two yachts cross each other's course, the one coming from the **right** has priority, except when **one only** of the two yachts is 'wind astern' or doing 'grand largne'. The 'non-priority' yacht must either veer away or stop. By 'grand largne' is meant the maneuver of going down the wind in a zig-zag manner to increase speed.

7. TURNING POINTS:

Turns are indicated by a drum or mound surmounted by a RED and WHITE flag. A white horizontal arrow on a blue background placed beneath the ORANGE flag indicates the direction to be taken (see also RULE 8(e) below).

8. OVERTAKING:

(a) **Beginning** Overtaking begins as soon as there are less than two meters (6 ft) between the bow of the overtaking and the stern of the overtaken yacht.

(b) Overtaking ends when there are more than two meters (6 ft) between the stern of the overtaking and the bow of the overtaken yacht.

(c) The overtaking craft is responsible for making the maneuver without hindering the overtaken yacht.

(d) The overtaken yacht must maintain a steady course or veer away and if tacking must do so in a normal manner. Nevertheless the overtaken yacht has the right to tack when it meets an obstacle, e.g. signpost, pool, soft sand, drain, etc.

(e) **180 Degrees Turning Markers: ORANGE ZONE**—Inside this zone a competitor may only overtake on the outside in relation to the ORANGE LINE or TURNING MARKER.

BOUNDARIES OF THE ORANGE ZONE

It is a triangle with apexes fixed in the following manner:

1. **INNER MARKER:** Indicated by an ORANGE flag. This point is situated on the course and at least 60 meters before the turning marker. The line between the Inner Marker and the Turning Marker is called the Orange Line. It may not be crossed and is defined by small RED and BLUE flags.

2. **EX—Center Marker:** Indicated by an Orange Pennant. This point is situated at least 20 meters from the Turning Marker and at right angles to the Orange Line, on the side from which the turn is approached.

3. **OUTER MARKER:** Indicated by an Orange Pennant. This point lies on the Orange Line when extended, on the Far side of the Turning Marker and 20 meters from it.

9. FINISHING

(a) **Finish of a Race:** Results are judged from the base of the main mast as it crosses the finishing line. The finish must be indicated to each competitor by a BLACK and WHITE checkered flag.

(b) **Cancellation of Races:** A. The Jury may cancel a race if it considers there is excessive pushing. B. Unless 6 yachts successfully complete the course the race will be cancelled. A YELLOW flag indicates a cancelled race.

10. MEANS OF PROPULSION:

If a yacht stops for any reason, competitors are at liberty to restart it so long as their actions cannot be construed as continuous or systematic.

Pilots may take repair equipment with them and can help each other. They can seek assistance from breakdown vehicles or can return to the start to effect repair.

11. CREW, BALLAST, RIGGING:

The number of persons on board, the ballast, the disposition of weight and the rigging are left to the discretion of the pilot, except when anything to the contrary is indicated in special rules for the race.

However, the pilot is expected to adapt the sail and the ballast so that he can observe the sailing rules and is expected to take every adequate precaution to avoid collision with other yachts, third parties and obstacles.

12. CHANGING OF YACHTS:

A pilot is not allowed to change his yacht during a race, but on presenting a valid reason may be authorized by the Jury to use another yacht during a series of races.

13. THE TRACK:

The Track is defined by turning markers or route markers. It is forbidden to deposit ballast or any other object on the track. Pilots not entered for the race, those who have given up and those who have finished the course must keep clear enough away from the track so as not to hinder either competitors still racing or the Committee.

14. FAIR PLAY:

All the rules of the race must be observed in a spirit of fair play.

15. INFRINGEMENTS:

Infringements of the racing rules are punishable by a points penalty. An infringement which causes interlocking of yachts is punishable by double penalties, and disqualification if the incident compromises the race position of another pilot or puts him out of the race. An incompetent competitor may be disqualified and ordered to withdraw from the race. Penalty points will always be added to a pilot's total points.

16. SUSPENSION:

A pilot, on the report of the organizers to the N.A.L.S.A. and on the decision of the latter, may find himself forbidden to take part in one or several International Competitions. National Federations and Clubs will be notified by the N.A.L.S.A. of such decisions.

17. RESULTS:

At the end of each race, after hearing the report of the Race Committee, the protests of the competitors, and after having applied the official penalties about which the competitors will be informed, the Jury publishes the results.

18. DELAY OR POSTPONEMENT OF A RACE:

The Jury is the only authority for delaying, postponing or cancelling a race. It will give its reasons to the N.A.L.S.A. or organizing body.

19. PROTESTS:

To make a protest a pilot must:

(a) Put down a deposit of $2.00 which will be given back to him if the committee recognizes that his protest is well founded.

(b) Furnish in writing precise details of the rules invoked to the Committee before the announcement of the results or at the time when he is informed of a penalty.

20. RECOURSE TO THE INTERNATIONAL FEDERATION:

A competitor who does not feel he has had satisfaction after having lodged a claim under Rule 19, may have recourse to the Federation under the following conditions:

(a) Put down a deposit of $5.00 which will be returned to him if the N.A.L.S.A. recognizes that his claim is well founded. In such a case the Racing Committee will also be required to refund the $2.00 deposited with them.

(b) To make the complaint in writing immediately to the N.A.L.S.A. delegate who will present his case to the General Secretary no later than a week from the date of the complaint. The President will ensure action is taken within two months of receiving it.

21. PUBLICATION AND DISTRIBUTION:

The above rules will be sent to Organizing Committees. The latter will see to it that the pilots have copies and that they understand them.

AMERICAN LANDSAILING ORGANIZATION RULES

General Data

Eliminations and championship events are held for Junior, Women, **Chubasco** class and unlimited class categories. Junior, Women, and **Chubasco** class will be held in accordance with **Chubasco** class measurement rules.

Eligibility

All members of ALSO or members of a landsailing club recognized by ALSO are eligible. The entry fee is $2.

In unlimited and **Chubasco** classes, provisions for Class A and B racing will depend on skill. To compete for the National Championships in the unlimited or **Chubasco** classes, you must qualify for Class A. To become a Class A sailor, you must finish in the top half of the overall finishing field at Rancho California. The last half of the Rancho California overall finishing field will automatically become Class B.

Class B sailors may improve their standing and move into Class A by finishing first, second, or third in any of the qualifying events thereafter.

All sailors must further sail in two out of the three qualification events to qualify to sail for the National Championship.

Due to the limited number of participants in the Junior and Women's classes, they will not be broken down into A and B divisions. Their only requirement for qualifying to race for the championship is that they compete in two out of the three elimination events.

Since the finals are a two-day event, the championships will be held on the second day with the first day's events consisting of a warmup consulation event, whereby the top three finishers in Class B may move into Class A for the championships.

Starting line positions for all races will be determined at the driver's meeting by a drawing. Drivers lowest number to windward. Should a driver not be present at the driver's meeting for any reason, he will automatically be placed at leeward end of the starting line.

Entry Blanks

There will be entry blanks for the qualifying and the national championship events. You must sail the machine you have entered with your entry blank but should a change of machines become necessary, notify the recorder of the change prior to a race.

During the series of events, you may qualify yourself for the championship for more than one category but you may enter only one class category in the National Championships.

2. MANAGEMENT OF RACES

General Authority of Race Committee and Judges

All races shall be arranged, conducted and judged by the race committee under the direction of the sponsoring organization.

All machines entered or RACING shall be subject to the direction and control of the race committee, but it shall be the sole responsibility of each machine to decide whether or not to START or to continue to RACE.

Distribution

The sailing instructions shall be available to each machine entitled to race.

Changes

The race committee may change the sailing instructions by notice given to each machine affected prior to that race.

Point Scoring

The winner of each race is scored ¾ point, second machine 2, third machine 3, and so on. A machine that withdraws or does not finish is scored one more point than the number of starters. A machine that is disqualified is scored two more points than the number of starters.

Series Scoring

At the completion of a specified series of races, the points earned by each entrant in each event will be totalled. First place for the series will be awarded to the participant with the lowest score, second place to the next lowest, etc.

For the purpose of defining **participant**, the name of the helmsman will be used and the award will be to that helmsman who accumulates the highest series score.

3. GENERAL RULES

The following rules should apply at all times when landsailing whether racing or not. When racing, infractions of these rules will result in a penalty of disqualification.

Basic Safety Rule

The helmsman shall, at all times, operate and control his landsailer in a manner to avoid injury or damage to himself, his own equipment, other landsailers and their equipment, other individuals, and property of

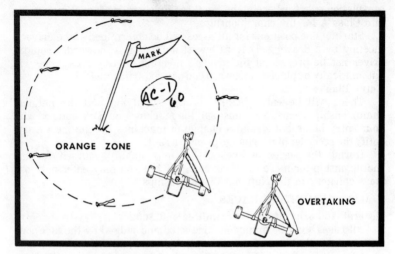

a public or private nature. Shoes must be worn at all times. Eye protection may be required at the discretion of the Race Committee.

Seatbelt Rule

When engaged in ALSO sponsored events, seatbelts must be worn at all times and, in particular, from prior to the starting signal of a race until the race is finished and the landsailer has been brought to a full stop. The only exception to this rule is when righting an overturned landsailer; in this case, seat belts must be refastened before the landsailer is again in motion.

Port-Starboard Rule

Any landsailer on port tack on any point of sail (boating, reaching or running) shall yield full right of way to any landsailer on starboard tack on any point of sail. A landsailer head to wind with sails luffing, when stopped, shall have right of way over all landsailers on any tack.

Same-Tack Rule

When two landsailers are on the same tack, the windward landsailer shall, at all times, stay clear of the leeward landsailer. Neither landsailer may, however, abruptly alter course in a manner to cause the other landsailer difficulty in keeping clear.

Overtaking Rule

When one landsailer is overtaking another landsailer, the burden of keeping clear and avoiding collision is on the overtaking landsailer. The process of overtaking is not deemed completed until the landsailer which was initially clear astern is clear ahead with all parts of his landsailer ahead of all parts of the overtaken landsailer.

Mark Rounding Rule

Each turning mark shall be surrounded by a suitable radius of orange markers (orange zone). Inside this orange zone, a competitor may only overtake another competitor on the outside in relation to the mark. The inside machine shall be entitled to sufficient maneuvering room to round or pass the MARK. No landsailor may touch any mark of the course during a race.

Any landsailer passing a mark on the wrong side or direction must retrace its path to pass the mark on the correct side.

Starting Rules

Seat belts must be fastened prior to starting signal.

No part of any landsailer may be ahead of the starting line at the starting signal of any race.

No landsailer may be in motion at the starting signal of any race.

No landsailer may receive any outside push or assistance immediately prior to or during the course of any race.

At the starting signal and until the "no assistance" signal, a period of five seconds, a landsailor may use his feet or hands to increase his starting momentum.

Finishing Rules

A landsailer has finished when any part of the machine has first crossed the finish line.

A landsailer which has finished shall immediately clear the finish line and stay fully clear of all landsailers which have not yet finished.

4. PROTESTS, DISQUALIFICATIONS, & APPEALS

Simple infractions

If, after a landsailor observes an infraction or possible infraction by another and informs him of same, the offending landsailer may (1) perform the two 360-degree-turn maneuver when clear and if not a starting, finishing, or collision situation, or (2) if he believes himself not in error, he may continue. The informal or offended landsailor then has the right to protest the action immediately after the completion of the race to the protest committee. If the protest is sustained, the offending landsailor will be disqualified.

Collisions and Major Infractions

In the event of a collision or major violation of the principles of sportsmanship, the offending racer may (1) withdraw from the race and

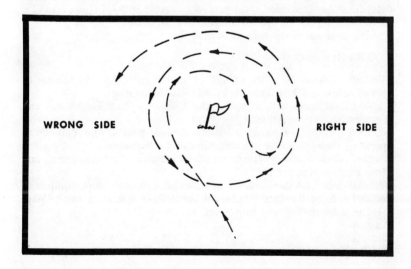

WRONG SIDE   RIGHT SIDE

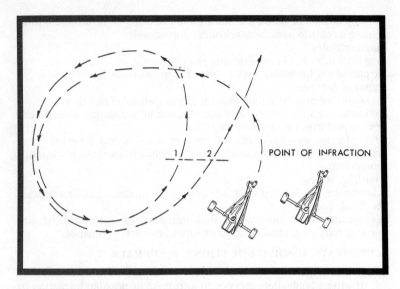

POINT OF INFRACTION

receive a "did not finish" score if he believes he was in error, or (2) continue under protest. If the protest is sustained, the offender will be disqualified from the event.

Handling of Protests and Appeals

In the event of a protest, the protest committee will listen to the cases of both parties together and shall decide the disposition of the protest.

The offender or offended may appeal the decision of the protest committee as follows: All participants in the race in which the protest occurred shall hear the case as stated briefly by each side without question, comment or discussion. The participants and the protest committee with the exception of the protesting and protested parties shall determine the disposition of the protest by secret ballot. In the event of a tie vote, the vote of the protest committee shall count twice.

The decision of the appeal is final.

5. ALSO Racing Classes

JUNIOR CLASS—15 years of age or under with the capabilities of operating his landsailer in a controlled and safe manner.
Junior Class Races will be held under **Chubasco** Class Equipment and Measurement Requirements.
WOMEN'S CLASS—Open to all women, regardless of age, capable of operating their landsailer in a controlled and safe manner.
Women's Class Races will be held under **Chubasco** Class Equipment and Measurement Requirements.
UNLIMITED CLASS—Open to any landsailors, with any equipment deemed safe by the race committee, capable of operating their equipment in a controlled and safe manner.
Class A
Class B
CHUBASCO CLASS—Open to any landsailor with landsailing equipment

which means **Chubasco Class** equipment and measurement requirements and that they have the capabilities to operate said landsailer in a controlled and safe manner.

Class A

Class B

Further racing classes may be added in the future as deemed necessary by ALSO membership.

6. Equipment and Measurement Requirements for Chubasco Class Racing

One-design races open **only** to **standard Chubasco** landsailing units. The term **standard** signifies that the **Chubasco** unit must conform to factory specifications in all significant respects including:

Sail design: Sail plan dimensions and area, battens attachment to mast and boom and may not exceed sail plan dimensions.

Mainframe, seating, tripod, steering, mast and boom.

Axle, wheel and tire assemblies.

Mast and boom, height, length, or diameter variations are permitted specifically as follows:

1.) Alternate arrangements of main sheet and sheeting system including location, number and type of blocks (ratchet blocks, four part and higher purchase system.)

2.) Outhaul and downhaul attachment and adjustment provided that no physical modification be made to the sail itself nor any adjustment be made during a race.

3.) Boom vangs or preventers are permitted.

4.) Tire pressure, wheel and steering lubrication.

5.) Forestays and shrouds are not permitted.

Appendix D
Ice Yacht Club Directory

CONNECTICUT

Bantam Lake Yacht Club. c/o Apley N. Austin, E. Shore Rd., Morris, Conn. Phone 203-567-5393. Fleet Capt. Lynn E. Richardson, 214 Westwood Rd., Bristol, Conn. Phone 203-582-3254. Ten active DN skippers. Club sails on Bantam Lake 1 mi x 2 mi. Facilities: Heated clubhouse with 200 ft front. Directions: from Rt. 8, Thomaston onto Rt. 109 to Bantam Lake (15 mi NW of Waterbury). Good sailing Dec 20-Mar 20. Lodging: Howard Johnson, Waterbury; Westleigh Inn, Litchfield; youth hostel, Morris. Contact for current ice conditions: A.N. Austin or L.E. Richardson, as above. Site used mostly on weekends, irregularly on weekdays.

New London Ice Yachting Club. c/o Richard Steinhilber, Commodore, 21 Sapia Dr., E Lyme, Conn. Twenty-five active DN skippers. Club sails on Rogers Lake 5 mi x 1 mi and Gardner Lake 3 mi x 1 mi. Directions: I 95, north of Old Saybrook on Post Rd. Good sailing Jan-Mar. Lodging: Connecticut Yankee Motor Inn, E Lyme; Red Lion Inn, New London.

ILLINOIS

Decatur Ice Sailing Club. Contact Fleet Capt. Vincent A. Langone, 359 S Lake Shore Dr., Decatur, Ill. 62521. Phone 217-428-7520. Twenty active DN skippers.Club sails on Lake Decatur, main basin 1 mi x ¾ mi. Facilities: ramp, shelter, fireplace. Good sailing Jan-Feb. Lodging: Lakeside Motel, Rt. 36. Contact for current ice conditions: Frank Castelli, Safety Director, 217-423-0857. Site used 7 days. Club hosts Illinois State Championship in the middle of January.

ILLINOIS-INDIANA

Illiana·Yacht Club INC.121 st St. & Wolf Lake, Roby, Ind. 46326. Ten active DN skippers. Contact: Matt Gornick, 9427 Ewing Ave., Chicago, Ill. 60617. Phone 312-ES5-0165. Club sails on WOLF Lake 1 mi x ¾ mi. Facilities: lakeside parking, easy launching. Directions: U.S. Rt 90 to Indianapolis Blvd. exit (106). Good sailing Dec 20-end of season. Contact for current ice conditions: M. Gornick, as above. Club plans to host regattas in future, will notify IDNIYRA of details.

INDIANA

Indianapolis Sailing Club. Geist Reservoir, RR No. 13, PO Box 283 C, Indianapolis, Ind. Twenty active DN skippers. Contact: G.S. Rian. Club sails on usable ice 3 mi x ¼ mi. Directions: 13 mi NE of Indianapolis on Fall Creek Rd. Good sailing Jan-Mar. Lodging: Holiday Inn, Meadows Motel. Site used mostly on weekends. Club hosts regatta in late January. All launching facilities. Year round club house seating for dinner for 250, bar available for special occasions.

Cedar Lake Ice Yacht Club. Cedar Lake, Indiana. Six active DN skippers. Contact : Pat Mee. Club sails on Cedar Lake 1½ mi x 7 mi. Facilities: private, limited launching site. Site used weekends and weekdays.

MASSACHUSETTS

New England Ice Sailing Association. Contact: Jim Bonney, Pleasant St., Metlon, Mass. 02186 or Stuart Nelson, 16 Bloomfield St., Squantum, Mass. 02171. Phone 617-773-4677. Twenty-five active DN skippers.

MICHIGAN

Gull Lake Ice Yacht Club. c/o Raymond E. Croasdale, Sec.-Treas., 2255 Idlewild, Richland, Mich. Phone 616-629-4414. Sixteen active DN skippers. Club sails on Gull Lake 2 mi x 5 mi. Facilities: drive onto ice for launch. Directions: I 96 to Mich. Rt 89. Lodging: Gull Lake Motel, Rt 89 in Augusta, Holiday Inn at Kalamazoo. Site used 7 days.

Detroit News Ice Yacht Club. c/o John Bush, 32457 N River Rd., Mt. Clemens, Mich. 48043. Phone 313-465-1639. Forty active DN skippers. Club sails on Lake St. Clair. Facilities: drive on ice for launch. Directions: I 94 to Metro Beach Hwy. Good sailing Dec 15-Mar 15. Lodging: Holiday Inn in downtown Mt. Clemens. Site used 7 days. Club hosts regattas, dates for this season not set as yet.

Cass Lake Ice Yacht Club. Pontiac, Mich. Club sails on Cass Lake 1 mi x 2½ mi. Facilities: use of Pontiac Yacht Club ramp and parking lot. Directions: U.S. Rt 24 to Orchard Lake. Good sailing Jan 1 -Mar 15. Lodging: Holiday Inn, Pontiac. Site used 7 days. Club plans regatta.

Lansing Sailing Club. PO Box 51, Haslett, Mich. 48840. Twelve active DN skippers. Contact : Walter DeGruyter, club address. Club sails on Lake Lansing 1 mi x ¾mi. Facilities: use of sailing club facilities with 60-car parking lot. Directions: 4 mi north of I 96. Good sailing Dec 25-Mar 15. Site used 7 days.

M & M Ice Yachting Association. Menominee, Mich. Four active DN skippers. Contact: Arlyn La Fortune, 615 Odgen, Marinette, Wis. Club sails on Green Bay, 20 sq mi, Little Bay Dt Noc, 2 mi x 7 mi, Lake Nocquebay, 3 mi x 1 mi. Facilities: drive on over public land. Directions: US Rt 41. Lodging: The Dome, Marinette, Wis., Menominee Hotel, Menominee, Mich., Holiday Inn, Marinette, Wis. Site used 7 days. Club hosts annual regatta N.W.I.Y.R. Assn.

Saginaw Bay Ice Yacht Club. 309 Martin, Bay City, Mich. 48706. Twelve active DN skippers. Principal Officer: Meade Gougeon. Club sails on Saginaw Bay 3 mi north of Bay City. Facilities: cars can drive off pavement 200 feet to ice and park on beach. Directions: exit I 75 at Wilder Rd., go east on Wilder Rd. to second traffic light and turn left on State Dr., take this to bay shore. Site used 7 days.

MINNESOTA

White Bear Lake DN Ice Yacht Association. Mahtomedi, Minn. Fifteen active DN skippers. Contact: Ronald Benton, 73 Tamarac St., Mahtomedi, Minn. Club sails on White Bear Lake 4 mi x 3 mi. Facilities: public boat launching site. Directions: Minn. Rts 61 and 244. Good sailing Dec - early April. Lodging: Jantzen's Motel. Contact for current ice conditions: William Ritt 612-426-3596 or 612-222-6644. Site used weekdays and weekends. Club hosts regattas occasionally.

NEW HAMPSHIRE

New England Ice Boat Association. c/o John Blake, Rindge, N.H. Thirty-five active DN skippers. Club sails on Massabesic Lake (Rt 121), Lake Winnipesaukee (Rt 11 or 28), Long Pond (Massachusetts). Facilities: lakeside launching, parking, Good sailing Dec 18 - April 12.

NEW JERSEY

Lake Hopatcong Ice Yacht Club. c/o Fleet Capt. David K. Nichols, 4 Powder Horn Grn., Sparta, N.J. Phone 201-729-7136. Six active DN skippers. Club sails on Lake Hopatcong, Budd Lake, Greenwood Lake. Facilities: ramps, dock, new site this year at Littels Beach, Chestnut Point. Directions: E Shore Lake Rd. from Rt 15 or Landing (Rt 80). Good sailing Dec 20-Mar 1. Lodging: Holiday Inn, Netcong, Ledgewood Motel, Rt 80. Contact for current ice conditions: D. Nichols, as above. Site used 7 days.

Hudson Highlands Ice Boat Club. Lakeside Inn, Greenwood Lake, N.J. Phone 201-728-1414. Seven active DN skippers. Contact: Werner Angrick, HHIC Fleet Capt., 195 Awosting Rd., Hewitt, N.J. 07421. Phone 201-728-3433. Club sails on Greenwood Lake 10 mi x 1 mi. Facilities: convenient launch site open to all visitors. Directions: Rt 46 to Rt 23 north to Echo Lake Rd. to Macopin Rd. Good sailing late Dec - mid-Mar. Lodgings: Binglie's Motel, New Continental. Contact for current ice conditions: W. Angrick, as above. Site used 7 days. Club has hosted EIYA.

Long Branch Ice Boat & Yacht Club. Patten Point, Long Branch, N.J. Twenty active DN skippers. Contact Dave Clapp, Little Silver, N.J. Phone 201-747-9549. Club sails on South and North Shrewsbury Rivers, Budd Lake, Round Valley. Facilities: launch off beach or at club. Directions: take Red Bank or Club Eatontown exit off Garden State Parkway. Sites used 7 days. Club has races every weekend, ice conditions permitting.

Shrewsbury Sailing & Yacht Club. c/o David Kingston, Gooseneck Point, Oceanport, N.J. Ten active DN skippers. Club sails on 2 mi course on Shrewsbury River. Facilities: launch via carry on, visitors welcome. Good sailing Jan-late Feb.

North Shrewsbury Ice Boat & Yacht Club. Marine Park, Red Bank, N.J. Commodore-John Larsen, 201-634-2030. Vice Commodore-Dan Davis, 201-493-4233. Fleet Captain-John Runyon, 201-741-0628. DN Fleet Captain-Dave Hadley, 201-776-5648. Chairman, 1972 DN Nat'l Championship Regatta-Tom Robinson, Sr., 201-747-4034. Chairman, Nat'l Sweepstakes Ice Boat Regatta-Skip Race, 201-291-1303. Fifty active DN skippers, Twenty-six Arrows. Five Yankees. Eleven Vikings. Sixteen Class A Stern-Steerers. Three Skeeters. Approx. twenty-five assorted small Stern-Steerers. Club sails on Navesink River, S.Shrewsbury River, Round Valley Reservoir, Budd Lake, Lake Hopatcong, Peck's Pond (Pa.) Facilities: complete clubhouse with sanitary facilities, workshop, carry-on launch, parking for 200 vehicles, restaurants nearby. Directions: Exit 109 on Garden State Parkway. Good sailing Jan-Feb. Dangerous spots marked by local club. Lodging: Trade Winds Motel, Sea Bright; Windjammer Motel, Sea Bright. Contact for current ice conditions: Dave Hadley, 201-776-5648. Sites used 7 days.

KENT ICE YACHTING ASSOCIATION

The Kent Ice Yachting Association is the largest organized Canadian DN club with a membership of 40 for the '71-72 season. The club is centered in Chatham, Ontario (approximately 50 miles east of Detroit, Michigan) and draws members from southwestern Ontario.

The Club has sponsored organized races for the last two years. We run 3 races each Sunday afternoon at Mitchell's Bay or the lighthouse on Lake St. Clair or at Erieau or Shrewsbury on Lake Erie.

The club has sponsored a Canadian championship race the last two seasons and this year will combine this race and the first annual Canadian International Invitational DNIYRA championship into one regatta the second weekend in February or one week after the International Regatta. All DN owners are invited to compete in this regatta and our regular races. The officers of the Club are:

Commodore-Robert Batton, 44 Cedarwood Cr., Chatham, Ontario Vice Commodore-Hugh McDougall, RR No 2, Blenheim, Ontario Sec. Treas.-Mrs. Charlotte Sparks, 46 Hillyard St., Chatham, Ontario. For further information please conact an officer of the Club.

NEW YORK

Lake Ronkonkoma Ice Boat & Yacht Club. Contact Fleet Capt. Reuben P. Snodgrass, 143 Lake Shore Dr., Lake Ronkonkoma N.Y. 11779. Phone 516-JU8-9569. Fifteen active DN skippers. Club sails on ½ mile course on Lake Ronkonkoma, 5 sq mi on Bellport Bay. Facilities: beach launch, visiting skippers need invitations. Good sailing Jan-Feb. Lodging: Eden Rock Motel, motels in Islip-McArthur Airport vicinity. Site used 7 days. Club hosts LRIB&YC Open DN (annual invitational regatta) in mid-Feb.

South Bay Scooter Club. Contact Bill Bannett, Sec. Treas., 140 Geritsen Ave., Bayport, L.I., N.Y. Twenty active DN skippers. Club sails on Great South Bay 2 mi course. Facilities: visiting skippers need invitations. Club hosts L.I. DN Championship restricted to L.I. skippers in mid-Feb.

Sodus Bay Ice Yacht Association. Contact D. Donald, 620 Shady Glen Cir., Webster, N.Y. Sailing sites used 7 days.

Onondega Ice Yacht Club Ltd. Contact Donald Dix, Van Antwerp Dr., Clay, N.Y. 13041. Phone 315-699-3465. Ten active DN skippers. Club sails on Sodus Bay 4 sq mi. Oneida Lake 20-25 sq mi. Directions: Rt 104 to Sodus Bay, Rt 81 or 31 NE of Cicero to Oneida Lake. Good sailing Jan 1-snow. Lodging: Bear Road Motel, 3 mi south of Cicero. Sites used mostly on weekends.

Irondequoit Bay Ice Boat Club. Contact Commodore Al Perrin, City Pier, Canandaigua, N.Y. Phone 315-394-1168. Thirty active DN skippers. Club sails on Irondequoit Bay 3½ mi x ¾ mi, Canandaigua Lake 15 mi x 1 mi. Good sailing Jan-Mar. Sites used 7 days. Club hosts regatta in early March.

....**Westchester Ice Sailing Club.** c/o Fred Moxley, Sec., 57 Dandy Dr., Cos Cob, Conn. 06807. Phone 203-869-1048. Thirty active DN skippers. Contact Commodore Robert Capidaglis, 6 Nesquake Ave., Port Washington, N.Y. 11050. Phone 516-883-6725. Club sails on Peach Lake, Candlewood Lake, Orange Lake and others in both N.Y. and Conn. Good sailing Dec 20-April 11. Sites used 7 days. Club has sponsored EIYA, also co-sponsor for Hudson Highlands, Orange Lake, and WISC Regattas and Hudson Centennial.

Orange Lake Ice Yacht Club. Contact Paul Sbraccia, Sec., Lakeside Rd., Newburgh, N.Y. 12550. Club sails on Orange Lake. Facilities: dirt driveway to within 50 ft of ice, then portage down slight incline. Visiting skippers welcome. Directions: I 84 exit 7N or New York Thruway Newburgh exit. Good sailing Dec 25-Mar 31. Lodging: Holiday Inn Rt 17 K Newburgh. Site used mostly on weekends.

Mecox Bay Ice Yacht Club. Contact Rod Overton, Walnut Ave., East Quogue, N.Y. 11942. Phone 516-653-5416. Eight active DN skippers. Club sails on Mecox Bay (650 acres). Directions: 2 mi east of village of Water Mill. Good sailing Jan 1-Mar 1. Lodging: hotels and motels in Southhampton. Site used mainly on weekends.

Hudson River Ice Yacht Club. Contact Ray Ruge, 4 Grand St., Newburgh, N.Y. 12550. Phone 914-561-7171. Club sails on Orange Lake 1 mi x ¾ mi. Club house right on lake. Directions: Rt 52 to Lakeside Rd.

OHIO

Sandusky Ice Yacht Club. 18659 E Shoreland, Rocky River, Ohio 44116. Fifty active DN skippers. Contact Bill Simonds, Sec. Treas., at above address. Phone 216-333-7131. Club sails on east end of Sandusky Bay 2 mi x 10 mi. Facilities: good launch facilities, parking. Directions: Ohio Turnpike or Ohio Rt 2 coming from east or west to U.S. Rt 250. North on Rt. 250 to Cleveland Ave. East on Cleveland Ave. one block. North on Ogantz St. to bay. Good sailing Jan 1-Feb 30. Lodgings: Holiday Inn, Ramada Inn, both on Rt. 250. Contact for current ice conditions:Bob Van Wagnen 216-288-8408, or Bill Simonds, phone above. Site used 7 days. Club hosts Lyman Invitational Trophy Regatta, to be held Jan 22-23, 1972. Entry fee: $5.00, registration Saturday, 12:00 noon.

Toledo Ice Yacht Club. c/o Robert G. Cramer, 5532 302nd St., Toledo, Ohio 43611. Twenty active DN skippers. Club sails on Maumee Bay 2 mi x 4 mi. Facilities: portable ramp over breakwall, parking in residential area limited. Directions: site is south of the Michigan-Ohio border, east of the Ottawa River. Good sailing Jan 1-Mar 1. Lodging: Holiday Inn, Rt 75. Contact for current ice conditions: R. G. Cramer 419-729-3213, R.C. Marleau 419-729-3358, or M.J. Holman 419-729-1773. Racing on weekends only. Club hosts no regular regattas.

Buckeye Lake Yacht Club. c/o J.M. Slaughter, 492 N Main St., Newark, Ohio 43005. Phone Newark operator, number is 344-5654. Twenty active DN skippers. Facilities: Launch over the wall, block and tackle on an overhanging track available, hanging dock. Club house where meals are available. Good sailing Jan 1-Mar 1. Directions: I 70 to Buckeye Lake exit. Rt 79 south to Buckeye Lake Park. Site is ¼ mi west of park. Lodging: Beech Ridge Motel, 200 yds south of I 70 off Rt 79. Contact for current ice conditions: J.M. Slaughter, as above. Site available 7 days, no organized races.

PENNSYLVANIA

Penn Lakes Ice Yacht Association. Butler County, Pa., Contact John Jombock, 2760 Grant St., New Kensington, Pa. 15068. Phone 412-335-8813. Fifteen active DN skippers. Club sails on Lake Arthur (Moraine State Park) 2 mile windward-leeward course on 3200 acre lake. Facilities: drive to edge of ice, good parking . Directions: 2½ mi east of I 79 on U.S.

422. Take "Day Use Area" exit of U.S. 422. Good sailing Jan 1-Mar 15. Lodging: Holiday Inn, others. Contact for current ice conditions: J. Jombock, as above, or Moraine State Park Hdqts. 412-368-8811. Club plans regattas in future.

Susquehanna. Wrightsville, Pa. Twelve active DN skippers. Contact George Sprenkle, RD No. 1, Wrightsville, Pa. 17368. Phone 717-252-2594. Club sails on Lake Clark on Susquehanna River, Safe Harbor Dam, Lake Morburg. Directions: 5 mi south of Wrightsville on Rt 624. Lodging: many on U.S. Rt. 30. Sites used 7 days.

Erie Yacht Club. PO Box 648, Erie, Pa. 16512. Twenty active DN skippers. Contact Dave Bierig, 955 W 4th St., Erie, Pa. 16507. Phone 814-528-3230. Club sails on Presque Isle Bay 3 x 1½ mi, various patches on Lake Erie. Facilities: launch from Yacht Club ramps. Directions: reach Presque Isle Bay from I 90 West to Peninsula Dr. or I 90 East to State St. Lodging: El Patio Motel, Scotts Motel. Contact for current ice conditions: Dave Bierig, as above, or Ted Sprague 814-725-1077.

WISCONSIN

Pewaukee Ice Yacht Club. c/o Bill Kuemmerlein, Commodore, 21500 W Doral Rd., Waukesha, Wis. 53186. Phone 414-782-3360. Fifteen active DN skippers. Club sails on Pewaukee Lake, "plenty of ice." Facilities: excellent drive-on launching, everyone welcome. Directions: Rt I 94 to SS, to PIYC. Good sailing Dec 15-Mar 15. Lodgings: Ramada Inn, Gulf Rd., Leilani, Blue Mound Rd. Contact for current ice conditions: Tim Fredman 414-462-9400 or Bill Kuemmerlein, as above. Site used 7 days. Club hosts PIYC DN Invitational, January 8-9. Perpetual trophy, 1st, 2nd, 3rd place keepers. Smoker on the ice after sailing.

Skeeter Ice Boat Club. Williams Bay, Wis. Contact Jane Pegel, PO Box 40, Williams Bay, Wis. 53191. Phone 414-245-6242. Fifteen active DN skippers. Club sails on Lake Geneva 7 mi x 1½ mi and Delavan Lake 3 mi x 1 mi. Facilities: launch by driving on ice over beach ramp. Directions: ¼ mi east of Hwy 67 in Williams Bay. Good sailing Jan 10-Mar 15. Lodging: Bay Shore Lodge, Williams Bay. Contact for current ice conditions: Jane Pegel, as above. Sites used 7 days.

Four Lakes Ice Yacht Association. c/o Paul Krueger, Sec., RFD No. 1, McFarland, Wis. Phone 608-838-3531. Thirty active DN skippers. Principle officer: Jack Loew, 3933 Hammersley Ave., Madison, Wis. Phone 608-233-6888. Club sails on Lake Mendota and Lake Monona. Facilities: walk on or drive on, for launch. Directions: West of I 90, three blocks from Wisconsin State Capital. Good sailing Dec. 20-Mar 1. Lodging: Holiday Inn. Contact for current ice conditions: J. Loew, as above. Sites used 7 days. Club hosts Northwestern Ice Yacht Association Annual Regatta in January.

Oshkosh Ice Yacht Club. 50 Main St., Oshkosh, Wis. Contact Marvin Luck, Sec.-Treas., Rt 2, Hortonville, Wis. 54944. Phone 414-779-6612. Ten active DN skippers. Club sails on Lake Winnebago 12 mi x 15 mi of ice, depending on snow. Facilities: unload on the ice. South Side Ice Yacht Club open to all, bar and club house overlook race course. Directions: take Hwy 41 to 26 East, then 24th St. to lake. Good sailing Dec-Mar. Lodging: Pioneer Inn & Marina, Oshkosh; Holiday Inn and Howard Johnson, Rt 41. Contact for current ice conditions: Gifford Gibson 414-

231-5762 or Pat Haverty Machine Shop 414-223-0120. Sites used 7 days. Club hosts Badger DN Regatta, January 9th, 1972, depending on lake conditions.

CANADA

Kent Ice Yachting Association. Chatham, Ontario. Forty active DN skippers. Contact Robert Barron, Commodore, 44 Cedarwood, Chatham, Ontario. Club sails on Mitchell's Bay on Lake St. Clair, Rondeau Bay on Lake Erie, and Erieau & Shrewsbury on Lake Erie. Facilities: launch from public sites. Directions: Rt. 401, approx 65 mi from Detroit. Good sailing Dec 25-Mar 15. Lodging: Bayview Hotel, Mitchell's Bay Hotel, Queen Motel, Holiday Inn. Contact for current ice conditions: Sid Garlick 519-676-5949, Harry Moore 519-352-2232, Boyce Libby 519-674-5790, Lee Sparks 519-352-5593.

WEST GERMANY

Eissegler-Gemeinschaft. c/o Fritz Herms, 3053 Steinhude, Ostenmeer 1, West Germany. Sixty active DN skippers. Club sails on Steinhuder Meer (30 quadrat KM). Directions: Autobahn Hanover, Abfahrt Wunstorf. Good sailing Jan-Feb. Lodging Pension Thiele, Pension Hansing, Steinhude. Site used 7 days.

EUROPEAN DN ORGANIZATION-1971

European Commodore-Gerhard Jettmar, 31 Udelweg, A-1110, Wien, Austria
Secretaries
Holland-Cees Kortenoever, Leeuwenlaan 295, S. Graveland, Holland
Sweden-Hans Bergkvist, St. Marietorp, S-181 31, Lidingo, Sweden
USSR-Heino Sisask, Vana OPostri 2, Tallin, Estnische, SSR
Germany-Klaus Muller-Seegers, 3053 Steinhude Meer, Schanze 12, West Germany
Hungary-Paul Sandor, Nepkoztarsasag U-3, Budapest VI, Hungary
Switzerland-Claude Lambelet, St.Honore 3, Neuchatel, Switzerland
Denmark-Hubert Christensen, Kirkevej 1, 2960 Rungsted Kyst, Denmark
Austria-Gerhard Jettmar, 31 Udelweg, A-1110 Wien, Austria
Poland-Tymoteusz Duchowski, Warszawa 45 U1, Kasprowicza 60 M 10, Poland

ALSO BY GEORGE SIPOSS

Model Car Racing...By Radio Control (**TAB** Book No. 592)

Index